How to Self-Publish in Oz

First Published – 2021
This edition published 2021 by Warm Witty Publishing
Sunshine Coast, Qld Australia
www.donnamunroauthor.com
Copyright © Donna Munro 2021

The National Library of Australia Cataloguing-in-Publication

Creator: Munro, Donna, author.

Title: How to Self-Publish in Oz / Donna Munro.

ISBN: 978-0-6480194-8-0 (paperback)

Subjects: Non-fiction,
           Writing resources
           Self-publishing
           Print-on-demand
           Australian writers

Typeset in Gill Sans 12pt
Cover artwork by Donna Munro.
Printed and bound in Australia by Ingram Spark

A catalogue record for this book is available from the National Library of Australia

How to Self-Publish in Oz

Donna Munro

www.donnamunroauthor.com

using this guide

This book originated from a workbook from an online course I tutored for Romance Writers of Australia in 2019. While compiling the course documents, I realised how difficult it must be for people new to self-publishing. There was no easy Australian-specific guide to self-publishing and print-on-demand. Yes, you can go online to find resources (and we'll get to them later), but knowing each step required isn't so straightforward, and most books gear towards America and the United Kingdom.

I wanted to help Australians intending to become self-publishers. That's you, right? You've chosen this book because you have a desire to publish a book of your own. *That's exciting!* When you hold your book, it will be a thrill like no other. I promise.

You may ask why I know this. And, good question. I tried the traditional rounds submitting to publishers and agents over the years. Time got away with me (you know the stuff, mortgage, work, kids, sport — *life!*).

After working in the small publishing and printing industry and becoming a graphic designer, I learnt a few useful skills. I started in the days of typesetting machines as big as a room. First, I'd print out headings in long strips and columns of text, waxed the back and laid out by hand, standing at an art table. After that, it was into a darkroom to produce the printing plates. Yep, I'm old school, but I taught myself desktop publishing on Mac and PC and continue to upskill.

Then, in 2016 I decided I couldn't wait any longer. At least one manuscript that was languishing in my filing cabinet needed to become a book, right? So, with this thought in my head, it was time for action.

I knew I could layout pages, design covers and send a book to a printer (don't worry if you can't — we'll get to that too). My time with a small publisher gave me insight into applying for ISBNs, sending data to libraries and marketing to bookstores. I had the skills, but even for me, there was a lot to learn. I took notes (resulting in this book). And, I suffered a few mistakes too. Even the most successful self-publishers, like Mark Dawson from *The Self Publishing Show*, made early mistakes.

Sorry to tell you there are pitfalls, but because I found some, you'll already be wary of them (and not fall far, and at least you'll have a soft landing).

In 2021 I have self-published three novels, this non-fiction book, and continue to work on book ideas. The dream is to write full time. I can see that day nearing (if I squint off into the distance with a heart full of hope). Anyhow, now it's your turn.

This guide is in four parts

Part 1 - The Dozen

Part 2 - The Freedom

Part 3 - The ABCs

Part 4 - Putting it all together (including links to awesome templates you can use in your writing and publishing business).

Work through each chapter.

Do the tasks? They'll be easy to find with this symbol:

Enjoy the process. So let's get started.

Contents

Part 1

The Dozen

The Dozen of Self-Publishing is a term for the number of essential elements needed to self-publish. They include:

1. Write
2. Drafts
3. Register
4. Marketing
5. Layout
6. Cover
7. Last Edit
8. Proof
9. Print
10. Distribute
11. Social Media
12. Promo Material

Chapter One
1. Write

Write the best book possible.

You can't self-publish a book if you don't finish your manuscript. Simple and true. Choose your style - pen to paper, fingers to keyboard, voice to the recorder, whatever way you write - get to it.

A finished manuscript takes the average writer one to three months to a year (or longer) to write, depending on the word count (and dedication). The more you procrastinate, the less chance you have of writing to completion. Begin today. Yes, I mean it - start (if you haven't) or keep going until the end.

I know you're keen to get this book finished, but how about you take a break now (yup, I know you just started).

Get your manuscript out (at whatever stage it is).

If you've finished, *yay you!* We're applauding. Please read your last chapter (to remind yourself how clever you are) and get back to the course and bear with me while I talk to the rest of the class.

If your manuscript is incomplete, read the last chapter you wrote (yes, even if it is chapter one). Are you ready to move to the next chapter?

Write at least three paragraphs of a chapter (the muse may give you the whole chapter, but that's okay. You can come back to me at any time).

Now that your head is back in your manuscript and excited about the possibility of it becoming a book, we'll continue.

The best way to finish a manuscript is to set yourself a goal. For example, write one chapter a day (approx. 2,500 words or any other word count you commit to).

If you write 80,000 words as 32 chapters (each chapter approx 2,500), you will aim to finish your manuscript in 32 days. So make your goal 40 days. This gives you some days for revision (or unforeseen things that may crop up, e.g., a child gets sick, the dog swallows a cane toad (if it does, flush its mouth with the hose), computer crashes. (*Hey, you did back up everything, didn't you?*)

It's a good idea to go over your previous chapter and edit it before starting the next one. Doing so refreshes your thoughts and often prompts the flow again.

I have a Book Publishing Progress Form with all stages of my work in progress (WIP). I'll share it with you at the end of this book. Fill it in as you move from writing to editing to publication and marketing.

Procrastination

Writers can often find anything to do other than write. They instead scroll through social media, bake a cake, eat ice cream, dip a spoon in a Peanut Butter jar (oops! That's me) or do anything other than writing.

Hard truth — not writing won't get your book written.

A book like *Use Your Words - A myth-busting, no-fear approach to writing* by Catherine Deveny may help. Or *The Writing Life* by Annie Dillard could inspire you to finish.

Hopefully, the table on the next page and the formula I use to finish a book will get your book written and ready to self-publish.

Question: How far along is your manuscript?

Task: Look at a calendar. Using the method explained (applying your individual timeframe, such as fitting in full or part-time work or other commitments), calculate an end date.

The sample formula is:

Book word count	Divide by	Words per day	Equals	Amount of Days	Approx. chapters
e.g. 80,000	÷	e.g. 2,500	=	32 allow 40	32

Word Count of Book (e.g., 80,000) divided by words per day (e.g., chapter of 2,500) = 32 Days (and approx. 32 chapters).

Set an end date for your manuscript.

My manuscript will be finished by	

Remember to set as few or as many words to suit your writing style. Every writer is different.

It's your pace. Your book. Your life.

Chapter Two

2. Drafts

Time to draft and edit

Okay, now, if you finished your manuscript in 40 days (or whatever goal you set), you must begin the drafts. (Oh, and congrats on finishing). Don't put your feet up on your desk yet. You have more work to do and many more drafts. That's right, get your bum back on the office chair and your feet on the floor.

Few of us get it right the first, second or third draft. Part of the creative process is to put the bones down (like a brain dump) and mould them into the story's body.

How many drafts should I do?

I often do eleven drafts or more. Each time you read through and edit, you'll find other things to change. For example, it may be that you've used the wrong tense or viewpoint.

Other stuff to take out are inconsistencies (don't spell a person's name differently or give them brown eyes when they were blue in the first chapter — unless, of course, they just put coloured contact lenses in their blue eyes). Eliminate redundant words like: then, that, and, very, really, so, got, get, just, had, was, were, etc. Sometimes they are necessary. You'll mostly find the sentence reads fine without them.

Take out clichés (there's usually a more interesting way to say something that means the same thing). Or put a new spin on an old cliché (making it — *well*, not cliché).

Don't repeat words too often, like starting each sentence with 'She'. Or use the same adjective or verb in a paragraph (unless necessary or while using for rhythm and pace). Delete most adverbs (ending in *ly*).

Make sure your sentence is in the correct order. Meaning, if you read it like this example:

I fell hard on my face after tripping on the cat.

Should be:
The cat ran under my leg, tripping me, so I fell hard on my face.

Because: the trip comes first before falling on your face.

Reading out loud
Reading out loud may pinpoint redundant words. It can also identify jarring passages you need to change, where words don't flow or dull words are putting the reader to sleep.
When you are happy with the final draft, don't be shy. Send it out to beta readers, critique partners, editors (if you can afford them) and anyone else who volunteers to read your work. When you receive the corrections, read through and carefully edit again. Don't be like me with my first book excitement. No rushing the process, no matter how eager you are to see your book printed.
You may be as keen as a kid during summer lined up for a Wet 'n' Wild slide, but you'll be disappointed if you find too many errors.

Text to speech
Like reading out loud may pinpoint boring scenes, so too can text to speech. This feature also makes you aware of where to delete or include commas.
In Word, highlight the passage you want to read. Click on the Review tab. Click the big 'A Read Aloud Speech'. The voice starts talking. You can pause, fast-forward, go back and stop the speech playing so you can make corrections to your MS.

Learn to love the method of drafting and editing. The better you get at it, the less of a chore it will seem. Editing is tough love. I look at it as the polish to your book. Gloss it right, and your book will shine.

Tips:

- Download the Grammarly app and pay for 'premium', ProWritingAid or similar.
- Read references like *Self-Editing for Fiction Writers, Second Edition: How to Edit Yourself Into Print* by Renni Browne and Dave King. Also, *Insider Editing tips for Self-Publishers: Avoiding Embarrassing Typos and Grammatical Errors* by Katherine Walden. There are plenty more.
- Put the manuscript aside for a couple of weeks after completion, so you see it in a new light when you read through it again.
- Use the spell and grammar checks in Word or other apps.
- Read your story out loud or use Text to Speech (if something jars, change it).
- Read the story backwards (not that I have tried this method).
- Be careful not to over-edit (find errors but don't take out the good stuff).
- Don't overuse certain words.
- Ensure you have not infringed anyone's copyright. Grammarly has a plagiarism tool. *The Self Publisher's Legal Handbook* explains further. Don't find yourself in a legal battle about your self-published book. Research copyright before you begin publishing.
- Don't use real people in a derogative way or make fictional characters similar to someone alive. They may want to sue you for including them. Get advice.

Editing List

- Line edit each word, sentence & paragraph.
- Check your tenses are consistent.

- Don't head hop.
- Use deep character POV (point of view).
- Balance narration, description and dialogue.
- Look for repeated words.
- Are characters weak or unformed (what is their goal, conflict and motivation)? Give your characters depth.
- Don't always start with he, she, they did etc., vary things.
- Stilted dialogue (people say, 'don't', not 'do not', unless writing historical where 'do not' is then correct speech).
- Find redundant words and cut them where necessary (then, that, and, very, really, so, over, are, as, is, up, down, had and it, etc.)
- Show don't tell (Not: *He heard a gunshot.* Instead: *A gunshot echoed through the air, loud and eerie.*).
- If there is a better word - find it.
- Boring scenes (unless you're planning to put your reader to sleep and your book is titled *Insomnia.*)
- Use your unique voice.
- Avoid clichés.
- Take courses on how to write and edit better.
- If you are writing non-fiction, does it make sense to the reader? Is it easy to understand?
- Use beta readers or critique partners.
- Pay for an editor if you have the funds.
- Use a manuscript assessor if you feel your manuscript needs more work.
- Use the services of writer organisations to find people to help.

Enjoy the process to make your book shine like a star.

Question: How many drafts of your manuscript have you completed?

Task: Find at least one or two beta readers or critique partners to read your manuscript and make comments. They will find things you will not see in your writing.

Chapter Three
3. Register

Your publishing process is nearing an exciting point. You've celebrated finishing your manuscript and now begins self-publishing. *Yay!*

In Australia, you will probably be a sole trader. If you are yet to do this, you can register as a business at:
https://www.abr.gov.au/business-super-funds-charities/applying-abn.

I registered Warm Witty Publishing because witty and warm resonated with me, and I intended to help others attain publication by sharing my publishing experiences. Working in publishing years earlier gave me most of the basic knowledge to begin my self-publishing journey (which I'm happily passing on to you).

You can use your legal name or pen name if you wish (making it your brand) as your business name. We'll discuss branding later. Once you have an ABN (Australian Business Number), you further the process of making your book real. In most cases, you'll need an ABN along with your business name, address and other details to register with a printer/distributor.

International Standard Book Number
ISBNs are numbers that relate to your book and the barcode on the back of your book. This number is how booksellers, distributors, libraries and buyers find your novel or non-fiction book.

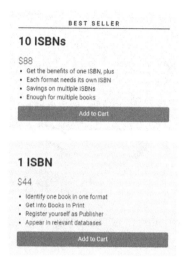

This pricing is current in May 2021 and may change.

Thorpe-Bowker's Identifier Services

Buy a batch of ISBNs at Thorpe-Bowker's Identifier Services. If you prefer, you can buy one at a time, but a bundle of ten means you can produce a paperback, ebook and audiobook (each book needing a unique number and barcode to enable you to sell it). https://www.myidentifiers.com.au/ $88 for ten at the time of writing in 2021.

Though, if you use Kindle Direct, the ISBN is supplied.

Do not buy from any other source than Thorpe-Bowker because other suppliers are only the middlemen. Thorpe-Bowker also has additional helpful, self-publishing information and services.

Keep a log of the barcodes and books (paperback, eBook, audiobook) attached to each. If you use Ingram Spark or have a barcode creator, you only need to purchase the ISBN, not the 'ISBN and Barcode' bundle (a barcode generates when you create a cover template with Ingram Spark).

Initially, I bought a batch of ten (you can buy individually). I used the first two for *The Zanzibar Moon* paperback and eBook. The following two for *Kendwa's Secret* paperback and eBook. See on the next page the table I use:

14

Warm Witty Publishing ISBN purchased 20.1.16

ISBN	Title	Type
978-0-6480194-0-4	The Zanzibar Moon	Paperback
978-0-6480194-1-1	The Zanzibar Moon	eBook
978-0-6480194-2-8	Kendwa's Secret	Paperback
978-0-6480194-3-5	Kendwa's Secret	eBook
978-0-6480194-4-2	Etc.	

There is also a table in the Thorpe-Bowker account on the ISBN dashboard.

Catalogue in Publication
Once you have your ISB numbers, you can register your book with NLA (National Library of Australia). I apply three months before the release, but if you are pre-releasing longer, apply earlier.

Go to: https://www.nla.gov.au/content/prepublication-data-service

Register your book's details. There is a user's guide. Please read it before filling in the details. The NLA no longer provide CIP (Catalogue in Publishing) details. They used to, but now it is up to the publisher to decide what goes on the CIP page. You will have to design your own, like the one I have included on the next page.

For example, for my book *Kendwa's Secret,* my CIP page details were:

First Published – 2018
This edition published 2018 by Warm Witty Publishing
Gold Coast, Qld Australia
www.warmwittypublishing.com.au
Copyright © Donna Munro 2018
     The National Library of Australia Cataloguing-in-Publication
     Creator: Munro, Donna, author.
     Title: Kendwa's Secret / Donna Munro.
     ISBN: 9780648019428 (paperback)
     Subjects: Romance fiction.
                Australian fiction.
                Contemporary women's fiction.
     All rights reserved.

Typeset in Times New Roman 12pt by Warm Witty Publishing.
Cover artwork by Donna Munro.
Printed and bound in Australia by Ingram Spark.

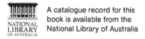

A catalogue record for this book is available from the National Library of Australia

These details go after the title page in your book layout. If you are unsure, study other books similar to your genre to decide where to put the CIP details.

Which printer/distributor should I use?

Good question. At this point, you should decide on your printer and distributor.

Sign up and register your publishing company with them. I use Ingram Spark https://www.ingramspark.com, and for the point of this course, I will use this company as my example. This is purely because the other alternative, Kindle Direct Publishing (once CreateSpace), does not allow you as much freedom (Amazon owns it). They no longer ship to Australia. In comparison, Ingram Spark prints in Melbourne.

You want to fly free in your self-publishing journey, don't you?

If you know of other POD (print-on-demand) printers, get quotes. I'll explain further in Chapter Nine.

As a self-publisher, I can't speak highly enough of my experience with Ingram Spark. Setting up your account is easy. They have plenty of explanatory videos, tips, checklists and manuals to help you along the way.

Go to their website and 'Create an Account'. As an Australian publisher, you do not need to pay tax overseas. Check anything you are unsure of with your accountant or tax agent. Ensure you have your ABN handy. You can ask as many questions as you like. Their reps help fill out your paperwork (of which there are multiple pages).

I recommend you also read as many reference books on self-publishing as possible. They don't always include everything specific to Australia, but they can help you understand the pitfalls. The most challenging being – marketing (we'll get to that later).

Research printers if you don't want to use Ingram Spark.

Other players are:

Reedsy	https://reedsy.com,
Draft2Digital	https://www.draft2digital.com
BookBaby	https://www.bookbaby.com
Tablo	https://tablo.com (more expensive)
Kobo	www.kobo.com/au/en/p/writinglife

They are worth checking out, particularly for ebooks.
Comparable to Ingram Spark, all distribute through Amazon and all

major book distribution outlets. Even by the time I go to print, there will be other options in the market.

Commercial printers can also print books, but unless they have book-printing presses for print on demand, the cost of your books can be high. They usually don't offer the same distribution channels either.

Do your research. Make a list of the things you require from your book printer. For example, do you want a paperback, ebook and audiobooks? Or do you only wish to publish ebooks? Whatever the requirements are, they need to be met by the printer or distributor.

This page includes a screenshot for you to understand the key elements of a book printer's website and what they have to offer the self-publisher.

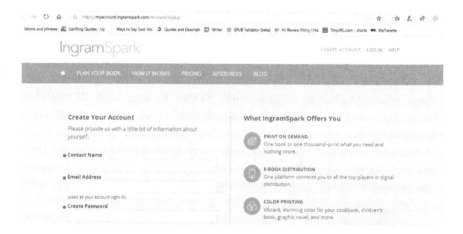

Be wary of vanity/subsidy/publishers who say they will do everything for you (at what cost?). Find professionals who provide the services you need (not the whole package). You may be good at layouts or artistic enough to create a brilliant book cover. If you believe you can do it yourself, you'll save hundreds, maybe thousands. You may even make money quickly after your outlay. Trust me — I did (not lots but enough to stay encouraged).

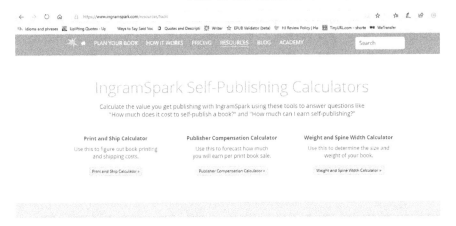

Pricing your book

Use Ingram's Print and Ship Calculator (or similar) to determine how much each paperback (you sell personally) will cost. Use the Publisher Compensation Calculator to see the amount of compensation per book sold through the distribution outlets (mostly POD) you receive. Taking these things into account, you'll be able to figure out how to price your book.

Draft2Digital also have a print ship calculator. They are another company like Ingram Spark that handle the POD and distribution for you. They specialise in ebooks and creating Universal Book Links with their Books2Read author pages. D2D is worth checking out as another printer/distributor option.

As a self-publisher, you set the percentage you pay the bookstore, but bookstores don't like receiving anything less than 40%. Some suggest setting a discount to 55% for bookstores to take up your book. (Booksellers are about profits, after all). I set mine at 50% and now use 55%, hoping the bookstores choose to stock the book.

Who gets what	Dollar amount
List your book price at	$29.99
Print charge	$10.24
Bookstore receive	$14.99
You, the author, receive	$4.76

As in the above example, if I list my book at $29.99, Ingram will take a print charge of $10.24. The bookstore gets $14.99. So you (the publisher) will only receive $4.76 per paperback sold. For ebooks, it's even less, approx 50 cents per ebook sold.

When you load your book file, you'll be able to set the pricing. Do the calculations and consider what other similar books are selling for before deciding on a price.

Compensation from selling through Amazon, Barnes and Noble, Booktopia, James Bennett, etc., is lower. Still, you don't have to do anything because they are POD (print on demand) or ordered from Ingrams. All you have to do is promote your book. You don't have to process orders, pack books and post them. That's up to the bookstore/distributors and the reason you receive less per book sale.

Library sales

Ingram and other distributors sell directly to library suppliers. Still, it's a good idea to approach libraries with an Advance Information Sheet (AIS) about your new release book and let them know they can purchase through library suppliers via Ingram.

I also contacted local libraries with my AIS. Sometimes, I wasn't approaching the correct book buyer, but I persevered until I had a list of the right people.

The National Library of Australia automatically sends your book details to Libraries Australia and Trove (after you've registered them).

You can approach ALS in South Australia, which has an online application www.alslib.com.au/authors. And James Bennett includes instructions and a form you can fill out about your book or books www.bennett.com.au/publisherservices.cfm. Let them know your book exists.

Question: Have you researched how you will print and distribute your book?

Task: Use the links provided in this chapter to study each option. Search for other printers and distributors who meet your requirements. Keep a list for when you are ready to self-publish.

Chapter Four
4. Marketing

You may wonder why this point is next. There is no published book in your hands yet, so why market it?

To be honest, you could have been marketing a year before your release. Build up the excitement for your readers. You need to let buyers know the book is coming a long time before you have a physical copy.

Often publishers will promote three months to a year in advance. It is the reason you design a cover now. It doesn't have to be the final, just an image representing the book (hopefully close to your final cover). We'll go into the cover in more detail soon.

Author platform
Build your author platform before your book baby is born.

Hurry up! You should have been doing this years ago.

If you don't have a blog, website or author page on Facebook, set one up now. If you are yet to build a website, you can create a free one on website builders WordPress (www.wordpress.com), Wix (https://www.wix.com/) and other sites. *Get to it.*

Later you can link your domain name to the website (e.g. yourname.author.com). You can also upgrade your site to add a bookstore.

The publishing industry talks about the author platform, but what does it mean? First, authors must be seen and known for readers to find their books to purchase and read.

How often do you hear someone say, "I love that author, I have all his books"?

Win a reader over with one book, and they are sure to go in search of your others. If it's difficult for them to find you or your books, plenty of other authors will try to push their books into readers' hands.

Author website

An author website is invaluable. You can use it as a blog or only have it as a landing page about yourself with a link to your books. Most authors title the website with their name. I agree with doing that though mine wasn't originally. I called my blog Warm Witty Words. Perhaps that was wrong of me, but I hadn't planned far enough ahead into my author branding.

I have registered the domain www.donnamunroauthor.com. And lucky I did. I discovered two other authors named Donna Munro.

Your author name or pen name is your brand. Make sure you brand well. There's plenty of help online for website creation, but if you want to try it yourself (those who are computer savvy), I recommend WordPress, Blogger, Wix, Weebly, Go Daddy, Site 123 and more (please note some costs vary per month/year). Choose the one that seems most straightforward and has the best features for you. There is also one that is designed for authors, authorcats.com and is a platform management tool also.

If you are not tech-savvy and can't set up your author website, pay someone to create one for you. You can find help through any of the above sites, Fivver and Airtasker or the domain sellers like Go Daddy, Hostgator, Crazy Domains and others.

On your author website, include these tabs:

- Author bio
- News
- Book info
- Bookstore (links to PayPal or Amazon to buy the books)
- Blog
- Media (clips from newspapers, podcasts and appearances)
- Media pack (bio, author questions, book trailers, press releases, contact details, author photo)
- Free downloads
- Podcasts (if you have any)
- Contact

Or, if you don't want a website, you can go on sites that let authors list their books like https://books2read.com, https://bookfunnel.com and www.goodreads.com/author/program.

Social Media

Today's writers need social media to promote their books and brand. It may seem a daunting task to post on these platforms regularly, but it can build your audience. Time – we all have too little – find ways to post in minimal time.

In WordPress, you can post your blog to multiple social media sites using Publicize. It will post to Facebook, Twitter, Instagram, and LinkedIn. There are scheduled posts on Facebook.

Using Pic Art, Canva, Adobe Spark, or similar apps allows you to post to Instagram, Facebook, Twitter, and Pinterest simultaneously and create beautiful graphics. There are other apps for multiple posts; some cost money, some don't. I use <u>Later</u> to schedule posts—others use <u>Hootsuite</u>.

While WordPress does allow you to use Publicize to share posts, tags enable people to find your posts on specific topics. Facebook doesn't use tags or hashtags, but other social media do, particularly Instagram and Twitter.

For Instagram, post-well-designed pictures, e.g., your book cover and a book quote, but also don't bombard your followers. Balance book posts with engaging posts about other things. I find excerpts from my books and place them above romantic graphics. I also take photos of the beach or my dog and post them. Add hashtags (#)—more on this in Chapter Eleven.

Book Cover

The book front cover will be your main image for social media and marketing. It doesn't have to be the final cover but one that conveys the book's story. You can use your design skills or find specialised book images, like Book Brush <u>https://bookbrush.com</u> who have all sorts of book marketing templates, e.g. book images (you add your cover), books with backgrounds (themed) and box sets. Create lots of pictures to use in your marketing and text, including when the book will be released, where it will be available, quotes, reviews, etc. Canva is another you can use for easy designs and has smart mockups.

Pre-releases

Before the book is available (or released), most author's books will go on sale as pre-releases. Pre-releasing ensures you have some pre-orders and also places the book higher in sales lists.

It works like this. You set a date before the release date for pre-sales. The longer, the better because the sales can build up and come release day, you have the orders sitting there ready to go. Each pre-sale counts as a release day sale (depending on bookseller), which can place your book in a bestselling top 100 in a genre category.

Mark Dawson and The Self Publishing Channel have a wealth of information about pre-sales and marketing.

Research how to go about it via your chosen printer distributor. Plan ahead to ensure your book has the best chance of plentiful sales.

Reviews

You can ask people for reviews or go to places like Book Funnel, Book Sprout and review blogs. Goodreads is an excellent place for your books to receive reviews from avid book lovers. On their website, you can create an author profile and add all your books.

Good reviews help sell books.

Marketing changes, so you need to stay on top of the latest trends. I don't know all of it and couldn't possibly try every aspect of it. I suggest finding book marketing resources to have the best chance of marketing your book and ensuring sales.

Advertising

There are so many book advertisers it's impossible to go through them all. The main ones, of course, are Amazon and Facebook. Many others can help promote your book by reviewing, advertising or both at a cost.

Some authors recommend BookBub to sneak into the bestsellers list by securing one of the advertising promotions spots. Securing a spot is costly, but the results may be worth it if you have the funds available (only if they pick your book). It's getting competitive.

But there are plenty of alternatives. I'm no expert on bookselling. However, people like Mark Dawson, Alessandra Torress, Seth Godin and Joanna Penn are worth looking up.

Other places you can advertise your book:

- BookLife (part of *Publishers Weekly*)
- Just Kindle Books
- Book Funnel
- Book Tweeps (Twitter)

- Instagram
- Reedsy
- Books2You
- Fivver
- Free Booksy
- LitNuts
- Book Raid
- Story Origin
- Romance Reads
- New In Books
- Book Adrenaline
- Book Dealio
- The Fussy Librarian
- Many Books
- And, don't forget newspapers and magazines.

There's a lot involved in advertising your book online, especially using keywords. Targeting your readership with keywords means you have less chance of wasting your advertising dollars.

Fabulous, insightful courses like Bryan Cohen's, Mark Dawson's The Self Publishing School, Ricardo Fayet (Reedsy founder), Kindlepreneur, Kobo, Kindlepreneur and others can teach you the best marketing and advertising strategies for book sales. Yet, another area you need to do your research on.

Newsletters

The newsletter can be tedious, especially if you have a manuscript to finish, but it's best to have one. It doesn't matter if you don't send it often as long as the content is engaging. In addition, newsletters can build your potential reader list.

Create a newsletter on sites like MailChimp, MailerLite, Active Campaign, Benchmark and GetResponse. Most are easy to set up but check the fees are relevant to your starting list.

Ensure you can create a landing page or pop-up on your website, so potential subscribers find your newsletter.

Joining Book Sprout or Creative Indie can enable you to newsletter swap with other authors. An excellent way for that author's readers to check your books out and vice-versa.

You may think it's difficult enough to write a book. Filling in a monthly (or more or less) newsletter can stump authors. So how in the world will you think up enough content to engage readers?

Don't worry; below is a list to get you started.

Things to include in an author newsletter:

- Chatty, interesting letter personalised to the reader
- Book images
- New book releases
- Upcoming books
- Events like book signings, talks and launches
- Author's creative process
- Fanart (yes, that's pictures of fans holding your book or drawing a picture of you) Check out Trent Dalton's Instagram to see some fans send him.
- What you are reading (promote other authors, and they may publicise you)
- Authors you admire (interview them or do an article)
- Invite feedback and reviews
- Pictures of where you write, places you enjoy, your pet cat tap dancing on your keyboard
- Links to your social media
- Where they can buy the book
- Podcasts or video links

Book Trailer

Do I need a book trailer? No, but it could be fun making one. A book trailer doesn't need to cost too much. You can buy the videos, images and music content on Evanto, Vimeo, Storyblocks, Dreamtime, Shutterstock, iStock, Getty Images, Pond5 and others.

Suppose you don't have a video editing program like Adobe Premiere Pro. In that case, you can simply use Animoto, Doodly (cartoons), Wibbitz, Microsoft PowerPoint or Canva to create an MP3 or MP4 and load it onto your website.

Media Kit

Media kit or packs are a terrific thing to include on your website. Journalists interested in you or your books can download the files (Use Microsoft Word so they can cut and paste the text). Never give them more work. Make it easy.

What goes into a media or press pack:

- A professional author pic (not a badly-focused selfie)
- About me (bio and contact details - *not your private address*)
- Call to action (join my newsletter or mailing list)
- Calendar of events (book launches, book signings, speaking engagements, lectures and panels).
- Social media links
- Advanced Information Sheets
- Book Release / Media Release
- Author interview questions
- Blog and blog topics
- Collaborations
- Other published works
- Book reviews
- Media clips
- Podcasts or videos (to show your voice and camera style)

Anthologies

You may wonder why I have included anthologies in marketing, but I have my reasons. Inclusion in anthologies can boost your writing clips, engage new readers, and improve sales of subsequent books.

If you've written a novella, find other authors in your genre and approach them about doing an anthology. If there are five or six other authors and some of them are already producing bestsellers, their avid readers may enjoy your story and eagerly await your next one.

You can also create an anthology of your own short stories or novellas and sell them as a box set or give them away to tempt readers to become fans. This is usually done as ebooks and boxed like this example of my soon to be released complete box set, now called *The Zanzibar Affair*:

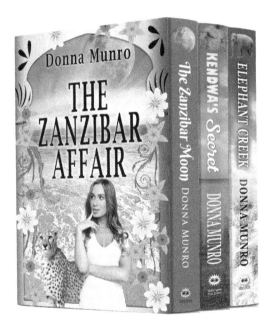

Question: What tasks are you yet to start on your author platform?

Task: Accomplish the setup for some of them. If you are not ready, research the sites I have mentioned. Have all the information on hand for when you are ready.

Hurry up – you should have been doing this years ago.

If you have built an author platform (website, social media, podcast, YouTube channel etc.), you're off to a great start. Hopefully, you already have followers who will convert to readers once your book is released.

Chapter Five

5. Layout

If you're a graphic designer, this part will be easier for you. I'll give everyone else a link to a Microsoft Word template I use for my books. Some of the book creation companies will have templates in a variety of sizes you can download. For example, you may want to vary the size from the average 152mm x 229mm to a smaller 111mm x 178mm for a novella.

Take great care with the design. I made the mistake of choosing a font I thought *looked pretty* for my first self-published book, *The Zanzibar Moon (sigh!)*. I returned to the standard Times New Roman 12pt for the next book. It's a standard for a reason, at least for fiction.

You don't have to use Word, but I'll explain the inside design with Word for the sake of this guide. Velum (only for Mac), Draft2Digital, Calibre, Reedsy and Smashwords (ebooks) also produce book layouts. In addition, many programs have layout features and can be used to design paperback books - including InDesign, Book Baby, Reedsy, and Publisher.

How do I know how to design my book inside?
Look at other novels to see what traditional publishers are doing and follow these layouts. You can choose a different font for chapter headings but navigate away from an arty-farty look. It won't work in the romance, crime, and thriller genres (though it can with fantasy, goth, and paranormal). Be aware of your genre. You don't want to stand out for a wrong design decision. It's preferable to make your mark by having your book blend with

traditionally published books and be known for telling a riveting story.

Decide on your book size by looking at other books in your genre.

Now you have your manuscript almost ready to be a book (*yay, happy dance*), you need to get it into shape as an actual book.

Laying out a book is relatively easy for me, but section breaks and numbering can be tricky (practice these before designing your book).

I have a Word template for 152 x 229 mm (6" x 9"), perfect for fiction. A5 is an easy standard for subsidy and vanity publishers, but it looks amateur. You'll see plenty of 6 x 9s on bookshelves. There are smaller sizes, particularly if the book needs to look thicker and more substantial. Most quick-read, novella-type books will be smaller too. It does depend on the sort of book you are producing. Ingram Spark, for instance, has over 30 sizes to choose from.

Regardless of size, there are a few things that you need to set up, like top and bottom margins, side mirror margins and orphan control. You'll add headings and page numbers. If unsure, at any point, Word has a handy help function. You can design in other programs, but writers most commonly use Word or Scrivener.

Adobe program InDesign can be the book-layout program if there are multiple graphics, but it is more complicated than Word. Vellum is an option (includes graphics) if you work on Mac. If you are using Scrivener, you will have to convert to Word. Whatever you use, you must be comfortable with it and capable of converting it into a printable PDF (later that is).

I'm going to stick to paperback books for this example using Word. This is because paperback books need a gutter to the left to be, what is called, perfect bound (glued flat to the spine).

This is how I layout my books in Microsoft Word:
Hit the Margin tab.

I set my top and bottom margins 1.4 cm.

The inside margin is 2 cm (this allows for perfect binding and a sufficient white area before your text.

The outside margin is slightly smaller because the binding doesn't hide it. I use 1.6 cm.

I then choose Portrait.

Mirror margins.

Hit the Paper tab. Make sure your paper is the size of your book you want to print, e.g. see the below screenshot.

Apply all those settings to your manuscript. It will start to look book-like. Like most writers, you have probably been typing your manuscript with double-spacing. Novels do not have double spacing (okay, maybe some non-fiction or children's books for readability, but let's stick to novels).

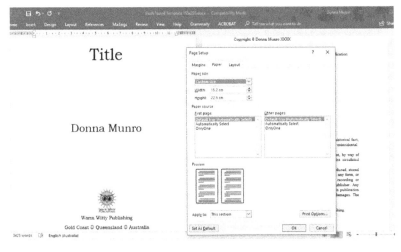

Set line spacing at 'exact' or 'single' depending on your preference.

For *The Zanzibar Moon*, I set exact 11pt because my font was 10.5pt Bookman Old Style. I loved its look but have gone back to 12pt (standard) single-line space in Times New Roman. You can use a larger font like 13pt for readability.

See, I told you I'd let you in on the pitfalls.

Though I initially chose Bookman Old Style, I found most publishers were sticking to Times New Roman. Check out traditionally published books to see how many are in this font. You may want to reinvent the wheel, but as a new publisher, agree with the inventors. Stick to standard fonts.

You will note, for this book (because it is non-fiction and more like a workbook), I have used a readable modern font Gill Sans MT in 12pt with chapter headings in Blacksword. Again, you need to check the genre (if fiction) or subject (if non-fiction) for your book's best style and font.

I have 'justified' the alignment. This gives a block look to the edges.

Indent the first line of each new paragraph by 0.5cm, except for the first line of a chapter.

Click the Line and Page Breaks tab.

Tick Orphan Control, so you don't have any loose words on a page. It's a personal preference whether to choose 'Don't hyphenate'. See the image on the next page.

Book layout style guide
A style guide allows you to check your layout is correct. I list the fonts and graphics I use. You can also add characters names, places, tricky spellings or use something like onestopforwriters.com to list those things.

See the following example of a style sheet:

Book Style Sheet

Heading 1 Part	**Gill Sans 28pt**
Heading 2 Chapters	*Bradley Hand 24pt*
Heading 3	Gill Sans 22pt
Text Headings	Gill Sans MT 12pt no indent/no indent first para
Text	Gill Sans MT 12pt No indent first para
Pics	Australia - titles Pen heart - chapters Hand with pen - tasks

You can add anything to a stylesheet, like spaces after parts and chapters — all things that you need to remember as you design your book.

There are more things you need to create the inside of your book.

Other pages may need inclusion:

- Title Page,
- Cataloguing In Publication Page (which includes the details you will register with the National Library of Australia at their CIP page: https://www.nla.gov.au/content/prepublication-data-service).

Pages that can be optional:

- Author Bio
- Dedication
- Map (if you are writing fantasy)
- Prologue
- Table of Contents (usually non-fiction)
- Quotes
- Acknowledgements
- Glossary
- Index
- Promos. I explain how to set up the basic ones (you can add whatever you want later).

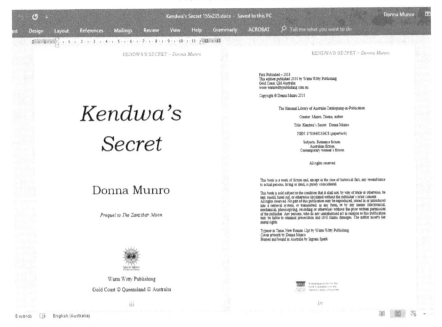

A sample of a title page and CIP page.

Title Page

Book Title, Sub-title (if you have one), Author, Co-author (if you have one), Illustrator (if you have one), publisher logo, publisher details. See my example for *Kendwa's Secret* on page 16.

Next is the Cataloguing In Publication Page (above screenshot). When you apply to The National Library of Australia, you must fill out details of your book (title, author, genre, readership etc.). They will send you back (via email) your recorded details. Type into your page as I've shown. You can upload their logo (I have placed it at the bottom of my page). You also need to include a disclaimer. Feel free to copy mine or look at other books to choose one that suits your story or non-fiction book. You can include the type of font used, the cover artwork designer, and the printer. Some authors keep it more straightforward, but I like to have all the information on my CIP page.

Author Biography.

A little bit of self-promotion goes a long way. Include your name, who you are, where you live (not your actual address, just your town or state), something interesting or quirky about you as a writer (e.g. my dog snores under my desk. Maybe your cat lies on your keyboard. You have a spider phobia but aren't afraid of sharks). Make sure it is brief and concise (approx. 150 words).

Dedication.

Usually a family member, someone you love, or someone who inspired you to write the book.

Acknowledgements.

You can include these in the dedication if there are only a couple. Otherwise, you can place the long list of acknowledgements in a new section if it is over a few pages.

Thank people like; editors, mentors, writing group, your snoring dog, and the postie (because he'll soon be dropping off boxes of books). Don't forget your best friend for lots of cuppas (alcohol and a shoulder to cry on) and your fitness trainer (for keeping your body from turning into a frumpy, sitting-in-a-chair-all-day author). I'm sure you get the idea, but don't be worried if you miss someone. You cannot write a whole book of acknowledgements. This is about you and your precious, soon-to-be-born book.

Table of Contents.

Are included if you are creating a non-fiction book. Yes, some fiction has a table of contents, like historical sagas and speculative fiction. The thing is, they can be difficult for beginners. So, unless you need one, I'm not going to go into it here (you can Google that one or use Word's help feature). See my example at the front of this tutorial.

Prologue.

Explains the past or goes back to another part of the story to foretell something exciting, interesting, intriguing or relevant. If you can include a hook, great. Make your readers want to continue to turn the pages until 'the end'.

Chapters.
Chapter number, Chapter Subtitle, Quotes (if you want them), the first paragraph has no indent. After that, each paragraph should indent.

Glossary.
If you are writing fantasy and have a make-believe world with many new creatures, a glossary is a good idea. Then, readers can flip back to it if they forget what something is.

Index.
Especially if you are doing non-fiction, not so much for fiction.

Promos.
At the back of *The Zanzibar Moon*, I promoted causes close to my heart (including photos) Umoja Orphanage Kenya, David Sheldrick Wildlife Trust and Africat. All had relevance to the book. At the back of *Kendwa's Secret*, I have a cover photo of *The Zanzibar Moon* and some of the lovely reviews I received from readers. Finally, I entered my website address so that readers could purchase either book and a teaser for the next women's fiction book *Elephant Creek*.

Book Clubs.
Book club questions can be at the back of the book. I included them in *The Zanzibar Moon* to entice book clubs to read the book.

Best Layouts.
I believe (and some may disagree) the best layout has each chapter starting on the right-hand page (odd number). This means you may have some blank pages on the even-number pages. If you are price-conscious, doing blank pages (where needed) may add a further 10-25 pages (approx.). I think it is worth it aesthetically for fiction. That many extra pages won't add up that much, sometimes not at all. I suggest you do the maths and decide for yourself.

About three months before you print your books, ensure you go to National Library of Australia's CIP page (stated in Chapter

Three) https://www.nla.gov.au. Fill in the relevant data. Your responsibility is to send a copy of your published book to both the National Library of Australia and the State Library in which your publishing business resides (within a month of publication).

Edit the book again.

Yes, that's right. Don't roll your eyes.

You've read every word, so often your head swims like a school of baitfish chased by a pack of sharks. Never mind, you're getting close to publication. Keep going.

Proofread and edit the book layout of your manuscript. Ask others to proofread to get more eyes on it. Have as many people reading as possible.

I found mistakes in *The Zanzibar Moon* after the first print run. I don't want this to happen to you. *Yes, again, I told you I'd tell you the pitfalls.* You can pay for a professional editor (if you have a spare $500 - $1300). The problem is unless the editor understands your genre and is a top-notch, structural and line editor, they may still leave errors in your manuscript (we're all human).

If you have the funds to pay a reputable editor who specialises in your genre, you're ahead of many self-published authors. Using one will take some of the stress of self-publishing away.

If you're not flush with funds, you can ask nicely (or use bribery like free books and chocolate) if your most well-read, literate family, friends, fellow writers could proofread for you. It could ensure similar results. Go ahead. Ask everyone. Try to have at least six to ten readers before you go to print.

Check all chapter pages start on the right-hand page (odd because we start with number one). Unless you don't want any blank pages. Ensure all chapter headings line up at the same point on the page and are consistent.

Check sub-heading, quotes, and paragraphs are all consistently formatted. Ensure all CIP information is on the CIP page and correct (especially your ISBN).

Add any changes from the multiple editors you have enlisted. Once done, go over the book thoroughly because it is easy to correct and replace with a misspelt word during your rush to have a finished book. After you've made any correction, read through the entire paragraph where the correction was made.

Grammarly is an excellent tool to help find grammar, punctuation, spelling mistakes, repetitions, passive voice and more. You can upload Grammarly at https://www.grammarly.com for free. I upgraded mine to 'premium' to have the extra features and apps a publisher needs, like adding it to Word (this checks my work as I type, though sometimes it runs slowly). I wish I had it when I wrote *The Zanzibar Moon*. I recommend it. It may be my favourite app ever! A warning, though; do not rely on it entirely. It is an assistant only.

Other apps Outwrite https://www.outwrite.com, Pro Writing Aid https://prowritingaid.com and Hemmingway Editor https://hemingwayapp.com are also grammar and spelling apps worth looking into.

Question: Do you understand how to lay out your book?

Task: Go to Chapter Twenty-Seven to download a book layout template in Microsoft Word for fiction and non-fiction books. Practice laying text into the templates.

Chapter Six

6. Cover

Hopefully, you already have a mockup you've been using for your pre-marketing. If not, you now need to polish your cover. Covers are one of the essential marketing tools for your book. Book covers need to reflect your book, genre and tone.

Again, look at other beautiful books for inspiration. For instance, *The Zanzibar Moon* cover had five covers I didn't consider professional enough. Though I am a graphic designer, this first cover stumped me. So I used Fiverr to find a book cover designer to get me started. She created it in Photoshop, enabling me to finish it off and tweak it until I was happy.

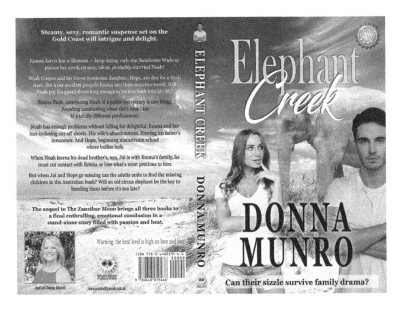

After learning better book cover design skills, I created the *Kendwa's Secret* and *Elephant Creek* covers using the Photoshop file from *The Zanzibar Moon*. Once I know the word count, I adjust each to the downloadable Ingram Spark template.

Most printers will supply a template, so your cover perfectly fits your number of pages, size, paper type, binding style etc.

Back cover blurb is one factor of a book often overlooked by publishers and authors (at their peril). The blurb sells the story as much as the front cover. Imagine a potential reader picks up the impressive, well-designed, intriguing book because of the front cover. Only to turn it over and read an uninspiring, badly-written blurb. It makes them throw the book down in disgust (yes, without even sneaking a peek at the brilliant first chapter).

What a waste of an opportunity! Fine-tune your blurb. I'll go into more about the blurb later. Most of your marketing and metadata will need the blurb, too (don't stress, I will explain metadata).

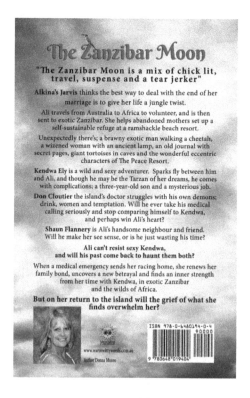

Images

Never Google search and copy an image. It can get you in trouble over copyright. There are plenty of places you can load free or paid images that don't infringe on copyright.

You can buy videos, images and music content on Evanto, Vimeo, Storyblocks, Dreamtime, Shutterstock, iStock, Getty Images, Pond5 and others. Again, and I can't stress this enough, make sure you don't infringe a creator's copyright. Ensure images you purchase to use on your cover (or anywhere in your book) are royalty-free and have worldwide in perpetuity. This means you can distribute your book anywhere, and your license never expires.

As a self-publisher, it is your responsibility to avoid litigation.

Question: Do you understand your genre and how your book cover should look?

Task: If you are not a designer, search for book designers who can show they know your genre. Get pricing. Choose the best.

Chapter Seven
7. Final Edit

Once you have the proof copy PDF, you need to check multiple things. Yes, another edit.

Let's call this one the *final edit* before receiving a paperback proof copy of your book.

Line edit through the book's inside pages using post-it notes (if you print out) or highlight (if doing so on-screen). This is also what you will ask your other readers to look for when proofreading. Primarily, you'll be ensuring there are no spelling mistakes and missing words.

Look for things like:

- Missing words or gaps in text.
- Check all chapter headings start in the same position with the same white space above and below.
- Ensure all chapters start on the correct page if you want them to be on the right (odd page).
- Consistent spacing.
- If using bullet points or numbering, they need to be consistent.
- Make sure nothing runs off the edge of the page.
- Are all indents consistent?
- Are page numbers correct?
- Ensure all images are the correct resolution.

Check the cover doesn't have any problems like:

- Words or images are bleeding off the page.
- Unbalanced type.
- Blurred pictures (wrong resolution).
- The spine is not lined up correctly with the cover or back cover.
- Colours look incorrect (RGB and CMYK can print differently from what you see on your computer).
- Headings and author names cannot be read from a distance (remember, your book image will be a thumbnail online).
- The blurb is not easily read and may need a different background to make it pop.
- The author photo looks unprofessional (don't have it looking like a badly-focused selfie).

Also, punctuation, spelling and grammar must be correct. Double-check that the ISBN is valid. Triple check the title and your name. Without due diligence, you can miss these things. Have other people proofread it. Call on your beta readers again. They probably deserve a bottle of wine on completion. I give my readers a free book and invite them to my book launch, and thank them in my speech.

It's exciting that your book release is near – but don't forget this is your project. You are the self-publisher. All errors left in your book are your responsibility. There's no buck-passing. You are it, not your book designer, beta readers, editors or other helpers. For the sake of your reputation as a self-published author, the final edit must be thorough. This is your brand. *Own it!*

Question: Do you take responsibility for your role as publisher.

Task: Make a list of people to approach to be beta readers (tell you what they like or don't like in the story), critique partners (fellow writers giving constructive criticism), editors (line edit or structural edit) and or designers (spot errors in your cover or layout).

Chapter Eight

8. Proof

You've designed your text in book format. The cover is complete and saved to the format your printer requires. It's time to load the files to your printer website. This is easy at Ingram Spark, but only if you have saved to the correct PDF type (usually PDF/X-1a:2001 or PDF/X-3:2002) for their files to work. Save your PDF with the Print to PDF feature so you can change the properties to suit what your printer requires.

Read all their manuals before you begin. The printer/or book producer will send an approval once it has loaded. Then, they will ask, 'Do you want a proof?'

Yes, you want a PDF proof (as stated in previous chapter) and then hardcopy (paperback) PROOFS – *definitely*, unless you are only doing an ebook or audiobook.

Currently (2021), Ingram Spark charges $49 for both eBook and paperback download of files. If you find changes in your proof, you may be charged a fee.

Some authors only choose the paperback option in Ingram and go to Kindle Direct or Smashwords for the eBook. This may give more control over the eBook discount deals (like in BookBub). But, again, do your research as to what suits you best.

Proof copies are vital. You've been looking at the manuscript for so long you can no longer see the errors and might even be going cross-eyed. You may have drafted and edited twenty times or more by this point. It's easy for your eyes to glaze over and your mind to be in la-la land dreaming of your book becoming a bestseller rather than proofread again. Hopefully, you will enjoy editing the proof copy. When that proof book arrives, your self-publishing process is coming to fruition. And, bonus, you get to hold your book in your hands. Yay! Happy dance!

I order five copies. One for me, and the other four, I post to my trusted proofreaders. Each reader uses post-it notes to show me where changes are necessary. When I received one with numerous post-it flags, I almost cried. Later, I realised how fortunate I was to have such a thorough proofreader. She saved my bacon when the book was finally published. You don't want new readers finding errors, but if your beta readers, critique partners or editors find them before publication, you keep your credibility.

It's your book baby! Give birth to a child you'll be proud of and want to show off.

Question: Do you understand the need for physical copies (paperback) of your book before publication?

Task: Make a list of people you can approach as your final book proofreaders.

Name	Email or phone	Date asked	Accepted or Declined

Chapter Nine
9. Print

Because you requested a book proof, your book details would have loaded metadata into the printer's system, including a blurb, author bio, ISBN and pricing (overseas as well as Australian).

The steps to download your files (to whichever book producer or printer you choose) will vary. Follow their instructions as you load the files. Most printers have manuals and instructions on how to save your files correctly. Study them beforehand to ensure you don't load incorrect data.

Make sure your metadata is correct. Metadata details are; author, book title, page count, word count, genre, blurb, reviews, and other relevant things. Metadata allows potential buyers, bookstores and libraries to find your book.

You're ready to publish once your final edit is complete and your new file uploaded. Use the print ship calculator to know how much each book will cost you (including delivery) to work out a selling price. To do this, click resources (you do not have to log in to calculate pricing, at least with Ingram Spark).

You'll find Tools under the Resources tab. Click Print Ship Calculator. Fill in the details of your book; ISBN, trim size, interior colour of paper (white or cream), binding type, laminate type, page count, ship to country, ship to province, ship to postal code, printing location (LS AUD).

For example, a 266-page book sized at 229 x 152 mm or (6 x 9 US) would be $6.57. If you calculate postage (you'll usually buy a whole carton). With standard shipping being $25 (under a dollar a book), your book's cost price is $7.57. Sell it for $20 and make a profit of $12.43 for any books you sell yourself. All, of course, depending on your book specifications (number of pages, size etc.)

There are plenty of other tools with book producing companies as well as help features. When you loaded the book, you would have set your sell price (mentioned on page 20). This tool is useful when you roughly know your word count. Recheck it when you load your last edited file ready for printing if you need to raise or lower your selling price.

You may find the cover is perfect, but some of the inside pages need corrections. In Ingram Spark, you can load each separately. Reload the corrected PDF. There may be a further fee, but it's better than errors in your book.

But what about your ebook?
Surely you're planning one. Don't shy away from creating an ebook. Platforms such as Draft2Digital and Kobo can help create

ebook files. If you want to do it yourself, the best program I have found for ebooks is <u>Calibre</u> ebook management. You can upload your Word file, check everything is okay and load the epub file to Ingram Spark (or wherever you are distributing it). Calibre's website has a video tour explaining how to use it, which is quite helpful. There's also a quick-start guide when you open the app, and it is free. *Yay!* (At least at the time of printing this book).

Calibre looks like this:

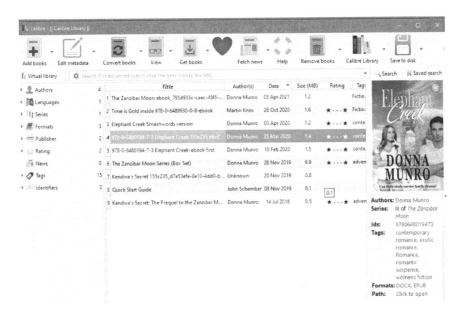

Again, you need to add metadata like your author name, blurb, tags, reviews and ISBN. Load the Word file, convert to an ebook, check the ebook is correct, make any changes, save and download ready to send to your distributor like Ingram Spark.

Now that both your paperback file, cover and epub are ready, it's time to order your first print run. Give yourself a hug (or let your favourite someone hug you). *Tada!*

Please note: there is more to printing and epublishing but it could take a whole book. For more details, download the manual provided by printers and distributors.

Audio Books

People are time-poor, and this is making audiobooks popular. Go for a walk, and you can listen to a book at the same time. It's another option for your book to be read (or heard in this case) by many.

If you have a radio voice, you could narrate your book on Audacity or something similar. However, recording at home can be tricky unless you have a soundproof room and microphone.

The Kobo platform https://www.kobo.com specialise in helping authors produced audiobooks and can provide narrators.

You'll also find narrators on Fiverr, Air Tasker and Findaway Voices.

Question: Are you going to publish in different formats?

Task: Choose the platforms you wish to use to publish your book; paperback, ebook or audiobook. Do your research on each.

Chapter Ten

10. Distribute

You have your book baby in your hands – now how do you send it to readers?

The beauty of POD is that the printer, in my case, Ingram Spark, distributes for you through Amazon, Booktopia, Bertrams, Barnes & Noble, Ingrams and others in the USA, UK, Europe, South America, Africa, Asia and more. If you can direct your buyers to these booksellers, they can purchase one book or more. Leading them is another thing.

Use your website or social media to build an email list of potential buyers. You can also have buyers pre-purchase (explained earlier). Some authors use Doc Forms on Google or similar for personal orders (signed copies). You only need to order as many books as necessary to fill orders. It's easy to set up a PayPal link on a website like WordPress or Wix, or you may want to have a shopping cart ready for when your publishing business takes off.

Book launch

Many authors hold a book launch soon after their book is first released. Due to a pandemic year, many authors now turn to online book launch parties. These can be organised by book promotions companies, Facebook groups and individual authors. Other authors, family and friends will join in to promote your book using giveaways and other ideas. Google some Book Launch Promoters to find out more.

I held physical book launches before the pandemic. Both were successful in selling to family, friends and a few readers. Books sold out during my first one, and I had to take orders for those who missed out. It may have been the novelty of attending their first book launch, or it could have been word-of-mouth (spread by readers before the book launch) that helped book sales. Either way, a book launch is a fun way to celebrate your self-publishing journey and the book you have produced. *It's worth raising a glass.*

A book launch is like any other event. Send invitations (even if it's online), cater to the numbers, set up a theme (e.g., jungle exotic for *The Zanzibar Moon*), ask guests to pay for alcohol (unless you can afford it — *I'll pay it forward when I have a bestseller*), and organise catering (nibbles are fine). You need to set up a signing table displaying your books, decorations and swag. Use pop-up banner, swag gifts and anything else to make the event memorable.

Sell and spruik

Always keep a book or two with you if you run into a buyer (and I don't mean run them over. We're all desperate to sell books but not that frantic). I sell copies while I'm doing the grocery shopping, dining out, socialising; you never know when you'll bump into someone who will want one. I always have bookmarks with me too. They have details of both books.

The books you physically sell yourself are not added to sales on Amazon and elsewhere. You might sell hundreds or thousands, but it will make no difference to bestseller lists. *Sigh!*

When you sell paperbacks and ebooks through your printer's distribution channels, those sales will be listed in your sales reports (issued by your printer/distributor). If you are an unknown author, these sales will be difficult until you gain good reviews and word-of-mouth.

You must be your own sales representative.

This doesn't mean your mum buying twenty books to give to family and friends is selling books. You want to find a readership. Start with family and friends, sure, but expand your horizons to your whole town, state, country and overseas. Don't be limited by where you live. Remember, print-on-demand can be as little as one book sold in Africa or thousands sold in Australia. Think extensive – distribute wide.

How do I sell to other stores other than book stores?

Try other outlets; newsagencies, fashion boutiques, small independent bookstores, pop-up shops in shopping centres, markets, libraries (at author talks), literary functions, book signings, fundraisers (you could donate books to build your brand), festivals, gift stores and outlets that work with your book theme.

I sell my three novels in a local news agency. Beach-read can sell at a bikini store (short summer stories and bikinis go well together, especially when on holiday). If you have a more erotic novel, why not try an adult store! Selling a thriller or paranormal, try a gothic trinket shop. Selling a non-fiction book on leaky taps, try a plumbing supply store. If your book is about the joys of drinking beer, set your sights on a brewery.

Selling in these outlets will be negotiated. The store may buy your books at 30-50% discount. Others may take them on consignment. Work out a deal that suits both parties. Give the seller a list of the number of books you are supplying so they can keep track of what sells, especially if they are on consignment.

Local markets may let you set up a store to sell your books at only a small cost — a cost you're sure to cover and make a profit.

If you haven't done your happy dance or raised your glass yet – do so now! Congratulations on self-publishing your book.

But we're not done yet.

Question: Do you have an outlet to sell your books?

Task: Write down at least five businesses you could approach to sell your book.

Business	Contact	Date asked	Accepted or Declined

Chapter Eleven
11. Social Media

I wrote a little about social media in the Marketing chapter. Now that social media has become *BIG* and a fundamental part of a writer's publicity and promotions, it needs a further explanation.

Social media platforms differ for age-group targets. Do your research or use the one that works for you already, but here are some.

Instagram. Instagram is probably becoming the favourite because people are time-poor, and images are quicker for engagement and to scroll through. As a writer, you want potential readers interested rather than flicking to the next post. Ensure all your posts have good quality graphics, and check each word before you post. Grammarly checks mine. Be sure to use hashtags (like metadata) to help people find your posts.

Try hashtags like (depending on your genre):
#booksofinstagram
#authors
#amwriting
#amreading
#suspensebooks
#contemporaryromance
#bookbloggers
#fantasy

Author and reader follow trains on Instagram can build followers. Yes, many of them will be other authors, but that's networking! If it's readers of your genre, that's even better.

Here's an example of a follow train:

😵 FOLLOW TRAIN TIME! 😵

Time to meet more great fellow women's fiction authors and readers!
😊📚🎉
RULES:
• Must follow ALL hosts @donnadmunro
@ anthealaureltonauthor
(your comment will be removed if not 😳)

• Like & Save this post
• comment Done and tag 3 bookish friends in the same comment
• Be sure to follow everyone who comments on your comment (Don't follow to unfollow, that's not nice 👎)
• Hosts will follow back at their discretion
• This post will be up for 48 hours before it is archived 👍
• Have Fun & Happy 'Meetings' Everyone!!! 🎊 📋 🎊
#bookfollowtrain

#followtrain

#bookstagram

#bookstagrammer

#readersofinstagram

#authorsofinstagram

#writersofinstagram

#reader

#womensfiction

#reading #author #books #bookish #writer #bookaholic #bookworm #booksofinstagram

#bookish #bookishfollowtrain #bookishfollowloop #bookishfollow #bestlifebooklife

Instagram users will follow you and your fellow author. You'll follow them back. If you have many people joining the train because they follow any of the above hashtags or are authors and readers listed by those participating, this could boost your followers by hundreds in 48 hours.

The reason for only posting for a small amount of time is that Instagram can ban users who suddenly get massive numbers. They may think you are artificially collecting likes or shares, using repetitive content, blah, blah, blah. You want to build like-minded followers — and particularly readers.

If you're smart about it, this is a terrific way to build your social media presence. And, you don't have to be the one who posts the train. Joining a train does the same thing, only not in as big numbers.

Don't forget to include a hashtag from your own book. For *Kendwa's Secret,* **I use**:

#KendwasSecret

#ILoveKendwa

#authordonnamunro

#warmwittywords

#warmwittypublishing

#donnadmunro

Think up some of your own.

Twitter. Shorter word counts can create a significant impact when worded correctly. Also, use hashtags, images and videos. I've found plenty of helpful writing information through Twitter. Use it for networking as well as engagement.

Facebook. Though becoming out of favour with some users, it can't hurt authors to keep an author page active. Keep your private page for family and friends and your author (or business) page public. Many features have upgraded as to what you can do, like slideshow videos with music.

I use Facebook advertisements to target readers. As far as advertising on either Facebook or Instagram, stick to a budget. Listen to what works for other authors.

Pinterest. Another visual social media outlet. People tend to create infograms as well as beautiful photos. Follow other author sites to see how you can use Pinterest in your best interests.

TikTok. New to the market, and I haven't tried it. If you're comfortable in front of a camera, you could give it a go. Dance with your book or sing one of your chapters? *Maybe.*

Of course, social media is a quickly changing environment, with new platforms forcing their way in. Some of the recent inclusions are TicTok (primarily for users under 30 and not shy about dancing and singing in a public forum), Clubhouse (a bit like Facebook and a podcasting mix), Caffeine (live group broadcasting), among others. Again, do searches to find the medium that suits you.

Mass social media marketing. Some platforms take the time out of social media posting. Later and Hootsuite both automate and schedule posts on a calendar to multiple social media channels. I use Later to use an image or video and text before posting to Facebook, Twitter, Instagram, and Pinterest simultaneously. It saves me time and is inexpensive.

Author specific marketing. Other platforms to promote yourself are specially designed for authors and book lovers, such as Goodreads, BookBub, AllAuthor and Book Funnel. Read the next chapter to find out more.

Question: Do you have a social media presence?

Task: How can you build your social media to find more readers?

Chapter Twelve
12. Promo Material

Earlier I discussed 'author platform', but let's explore further.

Do you need a website, or can you use something else?

As I said, your name (or pen name) is your brand. Splash it around on websites and other author sites.

Most authors will set up author pages on sites other than their personal author websites like Goodreads, BookBub, AllAuthor, WattPad, BookBaby and Amazon. You upload an author photo, bio, and profile details. Most of these sites will find your books for you to add to your profile. You can engage with readers and other writers through these sites. There's also promotion and advertising opportunities.

At a writer's conference, I discovered most bestselling authors talked about BookBub www.bookbub.com. It seems to be the best promotion for their books. Some offered their ebooks for free (during pre-release to gain readership). Others promoted their ebook at a price of .99c, some selling as many as 30,000 books during a promotion (*seriously*). That's good money (take into account the cost of the advertising). Also, it seems increasingly difficult to get a BookBub deal - worth trying, though. *Perhaps.*

BookBub also has a helpful regular newsletter, giving inside information on book marketing and promotions.

Advance Information Sheets and Press Releases

Email AIS (advance information sheets) to libraries and bookstores before the release of your book. Write one with the heading stating you are releasing such and such a book. It must be a teaser or a hook to get them interested. A blurb about the book:

include metadata like; book title, ISBN, page count, book size, book type, genre, publisher and of course, author. A picture of the book cover. An author picture and a small bio. You'll find samples on pages 100 - 101,

Press releases are similar, but you can add something about yourself that may cause a journalist's interest in you as the story rather than your book. Maybe you are a nurse, and you write medical romances, plus you also fell in love with a sexy doctor, just like the main female character in your book. AIS and press releases are a vital part of your author kit.

I sent a press release with details about the rescue of two circus elephants to promote *Elephant Creek*. Three local publications, one national magazine and a radio station picked it up. See the clip below:

An example of publicity using an interesting fact from a book.

Swag

I have bookmarks and pens to give out at signings. People love free stuff, making them a great marketing tool. Items like bookmarks, magnets, pens, mugs, mousepads, lip balms and other promo stuff you give away are called swag.

Some authors go to great expense to have swag for book signing and events. I'm not sure if too much of it entices more readers, but people love something for nothing. And, at least, it gets them near your books.

Swag ideas:

- Pens
- Notebooks
- Bookmarks
- Postcards
- Charms
- Bracelets
- Lip balm
- Glass cleaning fabric (printed with your logo)
- Cookies (with your cover on top)
- Cupcakes (with your cover on top)
- Mousepads
- Free books
- Business cards
- Tiny book cover chocolates (see next page)

I created my mini book covers in InDesign to fit in the smallest zip-lock plastic bag I could find at Officeworks. The front cover of *The Zanzibar Moon*, one side folded to *Kendwa's Secret* on the other side. I slipped five Smarties inside the folded paper and sealed the bag. This was a cheap, creative, easy way to design part of a book swag.

You could use the same concept over a toothpick and stick them on a cheese platter or into individual cupcakes.

Other things to consider when setting up for a signing with your swag (and books, of course) is signage. I have a colourful canvas banner that I drape across the front of signing desks. I also used my mother's art easel to hold a pop-out painting of my book cover, draping the easel with jasmine vines from my garden. I always have flowers (real or fake) to brighten my table and make it look exotic (like my books). Most authors use pop-up banners.

For signing setups:

- Posters
- Banners
- Pop-up Banners
- Fancy tablecloth (if not supplied at the event)
- Props like owls, typewriters, old books
- Books
- Flowers or other adornments
- Bookstands
- A4 clear stands (book promo info)
- Business card holder
- Brochure and bookmark holder
- A calligraphy pen for signing (plus a spare)
- Docket book for sales
- Notepads
- Square (or PayPal) so people can buy books if they don't have money
- A money wallet or petty cash box
- Sign-up form for newsletter
- Raffles (to sign up for newsletter)

Question: Do you have numerous ideas for promoting your book?

Task: Is there anything in the *Dozen of Self-Publishing* that you are yet to begin? During this week, try to accomplish some of them (at least get some ideas down). Research the sites I have mentioned, like Ingram Spark and WordPress. If you find any others write them down to add to the list in Part 3, like Zoom or Facebook launches!

Part 2

The Freedom

Self-publishing brings freedom. You have the power to decide what goes into your book, the edit, cover, marketing — everything. But, there are things you need to know. They include:

- Avoid the pitfalls
- Get organised
- Programs and apps
- Strengths and weaknesses
- Choosing helpers
- Extras to the Dozen

Chapter Thirteen
Common pitfalls

Avoiding pitfalls only comes with knowledge, like knowing not to get arty-farty for your layout or cover. It is wise to stick to what is commonly selling well. The more experienced you are, the better you will become.

Covers

Know the look for the cover genre. If it's a rural romance, there's usually land in the background, a handsome cowboy-hat-wearing dude and a feisty, pretty woman, traditional fonts, and soft or natural colours. A paranormal will be dark, vampires, tattoos, script type font often in red or purple. Chick-lit romance will be bright, with fun illustrations and stand out-funky fonts. Thrillers are usually dark, cryptic and with large sans-serif font titles.

Leaving out a review is a common pitfall. One good review on the cover (especially if it's by a bestselling author of the genre) will help with reader confidence. It can be on the front or back, wherever it looks best. The review only needs to be short but powerful, like award-winning author Michelle Somers has this quote on the back of *Simply Synopsis.*

'A Worthy investment that needs pride of place on
your writing craft shelf.'
STEPHANIE LONDON, USA TODAY BESTSELLING AUTHOR.

Inside the book

Inside it's best to stick to 12pt Times New Roman unless you are producing non-fiction. Again, flick through books in your genre, and you'll notice what is regularly published. Headings are larger, sometimes in a different font (not too fancy, unless you are writing a medieval fantasy or magical realism). Add some white space between the heading and author name. Always use cream (or crème US spelling) paper. White looks amateur unless the book is non-fiction. It screams 'self-published', and we want your book to yell *READ ME*. Keep to the genre-general look both inside and outside of the book.

Don't think you know it all

There is always something more to learn about self-publishing. Though I have written this course on self-publishing (and now the book), I am learning new things every day. I will always look for ways of producing books, ideas for marketing, places to sell books, conferences to attend, books to read (to help the craft). Be a sponge. Ask fellow authors how they self-publish.

It's not a competition with other authors

It's not a competition, so don't race against other writers. Complete your self-publishing journey at your own pace. Just because some authors produce a book every three months doesn't mean you have to. Admire other authors output but don't judge yourself against them.

If there is a part of the process you find difficult, enlist help by paying for a service (e.g., editing) or enlisting volunteers. Though you are responsible for all aspects of your self-publishing business, we can't possibly be excellent at all of it. I confess to being an improving editor, so I need outstanding proofreaders, beta readers and editors to go over my work.

If you can't design a business card, let alone a book cover, you need a book designer. When social media seems like a foreign language to you, ask for help. No one is perfect.

The biggest pitfall is thinking self-publishing is easy

There's a lot involved. It will get easier as you produce more books but don't expect every aspect to fall into place. You need to work hard at it, be meticulous and delegate anything you are not comfortable doing.

Some self-published authors do not conduct enough research before they begin. You need to know your market, where your book might sell or fit and who will buy it. My most extensive readership is middle-aged women and now (hopefully) other writers. What are yours? Do you know?

Other research is studying books similar to yours. How are some author's voices like yours? Is their book cover the style that would suit your book? Are they using gloss or matte covers? Is the book you are planning the right size for your genre? Before you self-publish your book, study these things.

Failing to order proof copies

Failing to order proof copies is another pitfall that sadly I fell into with my first book. It resulted in me finding mistakes in my first batch of books (I bought a box of 32). I uploaded a new file quickly but had to apologise to those who had bought my first books. Luckily, they still enjoyed the story, but it would have been ideal to find the errors before selling books.

Don't buy too many books

Have people sign up to buy your books, then you can gauge how many books you will need. Too many books gathering dust is not desirable for any author. With POD (print on demand), you no longer need to buy multiple books (unless you have a book launch or signing). Instead, buy books as you need to restock.

Use your money wisely

I pay for Adobe Creative Suite to design book covers and marketing material. Grammarly's premier feature is invaluable to me. You may want to splurge on Scrivener or a cover designer.

Create a budget. Know how much your book will cost once you've paid for editing, printing, cover, book launch, advertising — everything.

What can you afford and what you might have to wait for (until books make profits)? Some of you may want to spend your money on a good editor or book designer. Maybe you want to put money into advertising and promotions.

Plan what is money well spent and what is an indulgence.

Question: What are the pitfalls you may come across.

Task: Identify and list the pitfalls. Plan, so you avoid them.

Chapter Fourteen

Get organised

You work more efficiently when organised. I'm not trying to curb that creative bent where you plaster post-it notes over everything in your office (including the dog). It's more about the filing systems on your computer and in your office space.

Self-publishing is a business. It would be best if you treated it as such.

I'll share a list of the things that keep me organised. I tend to throw a wobbly fit if I can't find something when I need it (just ask my family), so having everything at arm's reach (or swivel chair) is essential.

You may need these things:

- Desk (one that fits your computer or laptop, pens, ruler, post-its, paperclips and other things you need close by).

- A small filing cabinet (I have a family-only draw at the bottom. The top one is for my writing business).

- A larger filing cabinet (where folders from the smaller filing cabinet are stored when they need permanent storing away).

- Document Trays (for as many jobs as you have at any given time).

- Ring Binders (best for keeping your receipts, sales, customer details).

- Paper (for your printer and for other things. I use different colours to code where a job is up to, e.g. draft, last edit, printer-ready).

- Cork or whiteboard (this can be either on your wall or a digital one on your computer). I like both and use OneNote.

- A gazillion notebooks (most writers collect these like bugs on a windscreen).

- Computer files (this is the most difficult to keep a check on, but I'll explain how I keep things in their place and easy to find). Don't forget to backup everything. See a sample of a WIP file (for *The Zanzibar Moon*) below.

- A budget (I have mine in Excel. You can use MYOB, Quickbooks, Xero or other free programs like Money Manager X and Free Accounting Software.

- Inventory list – I also use Access for this, but you can use Excel or similar (or within invoicing programs). Some authors prefer using a notebook or journal. Whatever works for you.

- Bookshelf, to hold your bestsellers, of course. Plus, I haven't met an author who doesn't love a bookshelf.

The previous page has an example of a typical book manuscript computer folder, '*The Zanzibar Moon*', including folders to keep organised. The only files I leave out of a folder are the book final in Word and the PDF file. I now add the ISBN to the name of each file because Ingram Spark requires it. So subsequent book files were, for example, Elephant Creek-paperback-978-0-6480194-6-6.

I have another two folders, Beta Readers and Editors, and each manuscript draft is inside the Drafts folder. In Admin, I keep book buyer lists, production plan, checklists and a budget.

You want to know where everything is at a glance. Something similar will keep you organised (at least on the computer). Perhaps you have a better system. Either way, find a plan that suits you.

But what if you don't have dedicated writing or publishing spaces or own everything on the list of things you may need? There are plenty of famous authors who wrote in coffee shops, sat at their kitchen bench or cleared out an attic. If you don't have the perfect office yet, don't procrastinate. You can self-publish without them. Whatever your space is, make it work for you.

Bookkeeping and Tax
I'm no tax expert, though I do go into some detail in Chapter Twenty-Three about keeping records. I believe in diligent record keeping. This way, if you ever get audited, you have proof of what you've spent going about your business.

As this is your business, I recommend seeking a tax agent or accountant who understands the publishing industry. Unfortunately, not all accounting professionals will comprehend the finer details of selling books worldwide. Check with your writer's groups for suggestions on the best people to help you run your business professionally and within our country's tax laws.

Question: What can you do to get more organised?

Task: Make a list of the things you need or what you have to do.

Chapter Fifteen
Programs and apps

I've attached a list of programs and apps that have helped my publishing story (or I found while researching how to do things for this book). They may not suit all your needs, but you have the information at your fingertips if you need it. I have used some of them extensively. Others I have only had a cursory glance. I suggest you investigate which ones may work for you as I would not endorse any above the other. They are merely suggestions to help your self-publishing business.

I have no affiliation with any of the companies I have mentioned in this list. It is up to you to explore which ones best suit your self-publishing business.

There are specialised sites to help authors like:

Showcase and promote your books

BookBub	www.bookbub.com
BookBaby	https://www.bookbaby.com
BookFunnel	https://bookfunnel.com
Books2Read	books2read.com
AllAuthor	www.allauthor.com
Goodreads	www.goodreads.com/author/program
Amazon	https://author.amazon.com
WattPad	www.wattpad.com
Kobo	https://www.kobo.com

Social media

Facebook	www.facebook.com
Instagram	www.instagram.com
Twitter	www.twitter.com
LinkedIn	www.linkedin.com
Tumblr	www.tumblr.com
TicTok	www.tiktok.com
Stumble Upon	www.stumbleupon.com

Book creation and printers

Thorpe-Bowker	www.myidentifiers.com.au
Ingram Spark	www.ingramspark.com
Kindle Direct	https://kdp.amazon.com
Smashwords (ebooks)	www.smashwords.com
Calibre (ebook)	https://calibre-ebook.com
Velum (ebook)	https://vellum.pub
Draft2Digital	www.draft2digital.com
Reedsy	https://reedsy.com
Kobo	www.kobo.com/au/en/p/writinglife
Zuma	https://zumapublishing.com
Findaway Voices	https://findawayvoices.com
Blurb	https://www.blurb.com (picture books)

Newsletter, press releases and sign-ups

MailChimp	www.mailchimp.com
MailerLite	https://www.mailerlite.com
Issuu	www.issuu.com
PRLog	www.prlog.org
Typeform	https://admin.typeform.com/signup
Google Forms	www.docs.google.com
JotForm	https://www.jotform.com

Images

Storyblocks	www.storyblocks.com
Pixabay	www.pixabay.com
Shutterstock	www.shutterstock.com
Adobe Stock	www.stockadobe.com
Dreamstime	www.dreamstime.com

Videos, slideshows and trailers

Animaker	www.animaker.com
YouTube	www.YouTube.com
Video Pad	www.nchsoftware.com/videopad
Smilebox	www.smilebox.com
Biteable	https://biteable.com
Animoto	https://animoto.com

Shopping sites and apps

Shopify	www.shopify.com
BigCommerce	www.bigcommerce.com
PayPal	www.paypal.com
Square Up	www.paypal.com
Books2Read	https://books2read.com
SquareUp	https://squareup.com/au/en

Websites and blogs

WordPress	www.wordpress.com
Blogger	www.blogger.com
Wix	www.wix.com
Simple Site	www.simplesite.com
Weebly	www.weebly.com
Go Daddy	www.godaddy.com
Site123	www.site123.com
Author Cats	https://authorcats.com

What books are selling:

KindleSpy	https://www.kdspy.com

Apps for book layout or plot organisation:

Word	https://www.microsoft.com/en-au
InDesign	https://www.adobe.com/au
Scrivener	www.literatureandlatte.com
One Stop	onestopforwriters.com

Apps for book covers and other graphics

Photoshop	https://www.adobe.com/au
InDesign	https://www.adobe.com/au

Illustrator	https://www.adobe.com/au
Adobe Spark	https://spark.adobe.com
Canva	https://www.canva.com/create/book-covers
Cover Creator	https://kdp.amazon.com

How to create and other info

Kindlepreneur	https://kindlepreneur.com/fiction-book-cover
Ingram Spark	https://www.ingramspark.com/help
The Writer	https://www.writermag.com
Self Publishing	Self Publishing Formula - YouTube
Best Page Forward	www.bestpageforward.net
Alessandra Torre	www.alessandratorreink.com

Question: Can you think of any more not listed in the previous pages?

Task: If you find more, add them to the list on the previous pages.

Chapter Sixteen
Strengths and weaknesses

As Sylvia Plath said, 'The worst enemy to creativity is self-doubt.' It applies to most writers I've met. If you let self-doubt halt your writing, you only have blank pages.

Writers sometimes wonder why they bother to write. We suffer from imposter syndrome and believe every other writer is waxing lyrical while we're spinning shit. Of course, it's not true, but the more we think about it, the more we believe it.

Even bestselling, award-winning, and famous authors have moments of self-doubt. They choose to ignore them and keep writing.

Perseverance is the key to overcoming any weakness. Persist one word at a time, one day at a time, until you believe you are getting somewhere with your publishing career.

Remember, some writers haven't even finished a short story, let alone a manuscript, and believe they'll suddenly become a famous author. A grandiose attitude won't help you either. Confidence is helpful but do not get full of yourself.

Approximately 97% of writers never finish a book. I hope being in the fabulous 3% who do, makes you realise your self-doubt needs booting out of your brain. You are terrific because you finished your book. And, you'll be super clever when you self-publish it, successful when you sell over 1,000 copies, and fabulous for believing and achieving your dream of self-publishing.

Keep things in perspective. Set goals and aim high, but you must know your strengths and weaknesses to balance them out for success.

Task: Write down your strengths v weaknesses in these columns. In the third column, write how to overcome weaknesses and build your strengths.

I've given you an example for the first.

Weakness	**Strength**	**How to overcome the weakness**
Editing	*Writing*	*Take time to do line edits*

Chapter Seventeen
Your helpers

When I finished my first publishable manuscript (I had another five in my filing cabinet. Let's call them my apprenticeship), I gave it to my mum and sister to read and edit. They are fabulous women and avid readers but being close to me didn't help the editing process. They were too proud of what I'd accomplished to be objective, even when I demanded they tell me if any of it sucked.

You'll find this with family and friends. Unless they have a true talent for editing and can be impartial, avoid asking them. You can use them as beta readers but not editing. Editing is complex enough without throwing relationship emotions into it. Find the best editor you can afford. Or perhaps you can swap something you do well for a fellow writer who is a good editor.

I swap book covers and book layout for edits. You could also write reviews, help market their book, design a book trailer or anything else you can trade for editing (and not your youngest son, though that is tempting, ha, ha! *Just kidding, Blake*).

Mentors are important
While working in book and magazine publishing earlier in my career, I was lucky to have writers and publishers encourage my dream.

I found a couple of long-established and successful authors with substantial (but kind) honesty and advice. They have been invaluable to my continued improvement as a writer, and I thank them for sharing their knowledge.

I belong to the fabulous Romance Writers of Australia. The support from fellow members has been the turning point for progressing in publishing. You wouldn't find a more giving bunch of writers; aspiring, emerging and established. I met a critique group through them and other wonderful authors who have become confidants. I also join local writers from various genres. We share the same dreams and meet regularly to discuss our writing progress.

And, if you can't meet a fellow writer in person, set up a Zoom meeting and chat online.

My closest friends don't get the writing gig, though most are supportive. Some mock it because they're going about their non-writing stuff and just don't get it! Don't let people discourage you. When you need encouragement, avoid anyone who doesn't understand or care. Find other writers or readers for support.

Whether it's cover design, book layout, website or marketing, any tasks you cannot do yourself, choose people who share or understand your vision. Research their work, double-check their credentials.

I once hired an editor on Fiverr. I've used the service before and have been happy with it. However, this editor missed a third of the edit, then asked me to give her a five-star review. *What the?*

My client (for a book I had ghostwritten) chose this editor from five I'd shortlisted. She's a spiritual/clairsentient woman and chose the editor because of a *vibe* rather than anything else. I'm not one to persuade her otherwise). Lesson learned, don't go off *vibe* — go off *research*.

After that experience, I would say it's better to check with other people who have used the editing service and see if they recommend that editor. This will give you a more accurate picture of their ability. Ask for a sample chapter edit first.

Be careful. Research your editors well, particularly if you are paying a lot of money. You'll pay anything from $500 - $3500 or more, depending on the word count and editor credentials.

I find the support of RWA is invaluable in finding recommendations for various publishing tasks. There are plenty of groups (both online and physical) writers can join. I've been a member of Queensland and NSW Writers at different times and plenty of Facebook groups. Find a group that suits the kind of writing you do, be it a thriller, fantasy, speculative, historical, contemporary, crime or non-fiction and where you feel at home. These organisations are there for you to pick the members' brains for advice.

Task: Start a list of the people you think may help your publishing journey.

Name	Email or phone	Experienced in	Could help with

Chapter Eighteen
Extras to the Dozen

As I said earlier, I would go into more detail on a couple of points. All twelve are essential elements of self-publishing. It would be best if you produced a well-written, polished story formatted into an easy-read book layout with a stand-out book cover (particular to the genre), with a blurb that perfectly covers the key elements of the story and grabs the reader.

The freedom is all yours as a self-published author. You pick your cover, layout, what to add in, what to edit out, your blurb, how you'll promote your book, whether you include a bio, book club, promotion or anything else. Each final decision is yours alone. Enjoy the liberating freedom of it but always remind yourself that your reputation is at stake with every decision you make.

Stay informed, network widely, listen to good advice, ignore the naysayers, improve your craft and take self-publishing by the reins. Ride your horse over the highest mountain (preferably off into the sunset with a hot guy/girl, whatever your preference), either in your stories or real life. *Aim high!*

Blurb and press release
We talked about these earlier, but I wanted to reiterate how essential good blurbs are because of the next task.

I read lots of cover blurbs to get mine true to the essence of the book. I wouldn't say I liked writing them at first, believing blurbs to be a boring part of book production. Now I enjoy them. *Go figure!*

A big reason for enjoying writing blurbs was reading Michelle Somers' *Simply Synopsis*. This book helps define your book's premise — another worthy addition to your business resources. It would be best if you created a blurb that catches the reader's attention.

Think of it as the elevator pitch. Exactly the essence of your story in a few words if you happened to run into an agent or publisher. Though, of course, you can spoil the ending with them, you don't want that on the book blurb.

Using your blurb, create an advanced information sheet or book release. Entice your readers by starting with a tagline/title to draw them in. Add your blurb and a cover picture. Place ISBN book details towards the bottom. At the bottom list where your book is available. My sample in the task is more of an advanced information sheet than a press release. It informs bookstores and libraries about the book release.

Below is my blurb from Elephant Creek:

Steamy, sexy, romantic suspense set on the Gold Coast will intrigue and delight.

Emma Jarvis has a dilemma — keep dating rock-star handsome Wade or pursue her crush on sexy, silent, *probably-married* Noah?

Noah Cooper and his Down's Syndrome daughter, Hope, are due for a fresh start. But a car accident propels Emma into their secretive world. Will Noah put his guard down long enough to let love back into his life?

Emma finds convincing Noah of a police conspiracy is one thing. Avoiding combusting when she's near him is a totally different predicament.

Noah has enough problems without falling for delightful Emma and her lust-inducing cut-off shorts. His wife's abandonment. Proving his father's innocence. And Hope, beginning mainstream school where bullies lurk.

When Noah learns his dead brother's son, Jai, is with Emma's family, he must cut contact with Emma or lose what's most precious to him.

But when Jai and Hope go missing, can the adults unite to find the missing children in the Australian bush? Will an old circus elephant be the key to bonding them before it's too late?

The sequel to The Zanzibar Moon brings all three books to a final enthralling, emotional conclusion in a stand-alone story filled with passion and heat.

Yes, I could have included a review, too. Sadly I didn't.

Task: Write and design an AIS for your story. I've given an example from *Kendwa's Secret* and the elements to include on the next page.
See my sample:

Kendwa's Secret – secrets, lies, love and betrayal in exotic locations

*"The prequel to **The Zanzibar Moon** lives up to its sexy expectations."*

Readers loved Kendwa so much they asked to read about his earlier life. Donna Munro has once again written in an easy-to-read engaging voice. There's plenty of passion in wild exotic settings; from Australia, Borneo, USA, England, Africa to the mysterious island of Zanzibar. What secrets are being kept?

Sexy crocodile wrangler and wildlife ranger **Kendwa Ely's** troubles didn't begin when he buried his parents; they started long before that.

In Africa, he is seven-years-old when the unthinkable happens, and he must stay silent. The years don't dim the secret. In a constant effort to forget it, he travels the world, wrangling crocodiles in Australia's Northern Territory, roping live alligators out of rich people's pools in Florida, fighting for eco-tourism and bedding a constant stream of women.

That is until he meets Sharli Ahu.

Exquisite as a Hindu princess, Sharli has values, humility, and beliefs. A strong, resourceful woman, she doesn't need a man like Kendwa. Borneo's orangutans are her priority.

But there's something about Kendwa. Even when he stuffs up, there's something sincere, strong and kind about him. But there are more important things in life than lusting after a wild guy like Kendwa.

In the jungles of Borneo, a venomous snake strikes and Sharli may be the only one who can save him.

Can their love grow, or will the shadow of his secret always be looming? Is it the catalyst for his biggest betrayal yet, or can he save the people he loves most?
Can true love survive the secrets people keep?

ISBN: 9780648019428 (paperback)	ISBN: 9780648019435 (eBook)
RRP: $25.99	RRP: $4.99
AUTHOR: Donna Munro	AUTHOR: Donna Munro
PUBLISHER: Warm Witty Publishing	PUBLISHER: Warm Witty Publishing
RELEASE DUE: August 2018	RELEASE DUE: July 2018

Purchase from all good bookstores including:
Amazon, Barnes & Noble, The Book Depository, Bertrams, Gardners, Booktopia, Fishpond, James Bennett, ALS and Peter Pal.

Purchase directly for signed author copies at:
www.warmwittywords.com.au/bookstore

Part 3

The ABCs

The ABSs are the final piece of the self-publishing puzzle for Australian writers. They include:

- Aptitude
- Belief
- Creativity

Chapter Nineteen
A - Aptitude

Aptitude is a skill, gift, capacity and ability. Being keen to take this course proves you have the interest, along with a manuscript ready to self-publish (or close to it).

Why are we celebrating before your book is published? Remember that a staggering 97% of writers who begin a novel never finish it. You're going to finish yours — celebrate that. You know (with certainty) you will. I have faith in you. Have belief in yourself.

You have calculated how long it would take to be written, given yourself a deadline, and wrote to completion (or close to it). Each time you make a milestone (e.g., chapter 12 is complete), buy yourself a new notebook, outfit, a bottle of wine, book, or ask your partner to take you out to dinner to celebrate by candlelight. Or just give yourself time out to relax with a book, have a bubble bath, do yoga or go to the beach.

Not many of us will win a Vogel or Booker, have Ellen interview us, end up featured in Reese's Book Club, or even snag a Tracey Grimshaw interview on Today Tonight, but we can be successful in our own right. *Own it!*

Your **aptitude** *is awesome!* Pat yourself on the back.

Task: Since aptitude is a skill, gift, capacity and ability, what is yours? What makes you capable of self-publishing well, and how do you feel about it?

Chapter Twenty
B - Belief

If you don't believe your talent, no one else will. As I already said, self-doubt kills creativity. It can make you stop your book project and toss it in a wheelie bin.

Have you written articles or short stories? You finished them - how talented are you? *Very.* Your talent will also help you write your book-length story or non-fiction book to completion - ready for you to self-publish. Your talent and belief in it will aid you during your self-publishing journey.

Sometimes you will be writing, and you think it's not good enough as you review your work. You compare yourself to other writers and believe your words aren't as beautifully written. But – what if they are? Perhaps they are even better. You're just not believing in your talent. Don't do this. Yes, fix writing that needs fixing (we all have to do that) but embrace the beautiful phrases you've thought up and written.

You may have doubted you could self-publish before you read this book, but now you've given yourself the tools to do so. Follow the steps in this guide and believe in your self-publishing success.

It's understandable to fluctuate from fear and doubt to hope and belief. To stay confident in your writing project, you need to change your mindset. Daily mantras and goal setting can help. Trust this self-publishing journey is your unique voyage.

Enjoy when you have a brilliant idea. Roll that incredible piece of dialogue on your tongue. When your characters have become so real you feel like a voyeur observing their heated discussions (and perhaps bedroom scenes or a crime), praise your ability. After you've designed a fabulous book cover that looks traditionally published, honour your talent and celebrate.

I take my books to department stores like Kmart and place them on the shelf next to similar titles. They look just as good. That makes me proud and able to believe in myself.

No one creates precisely like you. You have a unique voice and various other abilities.

This is your talent – *believe it.*

Yell it now, "My talent is awesome, and I believe in it."

Remind yourself of it every morning you wake. Use the following writing mantras as often as you like.

Your **belief** *in your talent is amazing!* Cheer yourself by raising a glass of bubbly (water, tea, coffee or whatever your poison).

Task: Use Canva, Adobe Spark or something else to create inspirational mantras that will help you believe in yourself. Post them to social media, pin them to a pinboard or somewhere you will see them often.

Chapter Twenty-One
Creativity

Writers are creative beings.

We conjure words from thin air. They float in our head, flow down to our fingers and end up being typed or written to form sentences, paragraphs, chapters and whole novels. If you have a day where the creativity is not flowing enough to write a sentence, let alone a chapter, stop writing and do something else.

Go for a walk. Admire budding flowers, breathe in their fragrance. Enjoy the sun on your face. Feel, touch, smell, see and hear what surrounds you. Suddenly storylines will form in your head. Hopefully, you have a notebook at hand (always have one or use the recording or note feature on your phone). Jot the ideas down.

If, for some reason, that doesn't work, try something creative that isn't writing. Paint, sew, garden, dance, build furniture - anything. As you do it, think about the story of what you are doing. You're staring at the old desk you repainted. It once belonged to a famous writer, which gets you imagining what it would be like to have lived in a different era. Story ideas form from random things.

Many things can spark creativity. For example, if you've finished the novel or non-fiction book and it's the cover you are stuck on, remember you were creative enough to write the book. You will be able to decide on a cover design.

Go to a bookstore or library for inspiration. Browse. Touch, smell, feel and see each book. Look at them from a distance. What pops out at you? Could this lead to a creative idea for your book cover?

Creativity often leads to creativity. Embrace yours.

You are absolutely brilliantly **creative**. Treat yourself by buying a book you want to read.

Task: Design a motivating sign to hang in your office based on the ABCs of self-publishing - Aptitude, Belief and Creativity. Something like the one on this page:

I have an awesome *Aptitude* for writing and publishing My *Belief* in my ability is total. *Creativity* comes from my heart.

Part 4

Putting it all together

The final piece of the self-publishing puzzle for Australian writers are the documents and checklists you'll need for your business to thrive. They include:

- Checklists
- Keeping records
- Future plans
- The last word
- Free templates

Chapter Twenty-Two
Checklists

I have attached a helpful checklist you can use in your self-publishing process so that your book looks like it is traditionally published. I've left lines at the bottom so you can add any new ones you discover during your progress.

Use this checklist along with my Book Publishing Progress Report (you can download it) to keep track of each book you self-publish. The list below is also available as a download.

Self-Publishing Checklist

Register as a business	☐
Establish manuscript finish date	☐
Start writing	☐
Buy ISBNs	☐
Contact or register with printer	☐
Finish writing	☐
Design cover for marketing	☐
Begin marketing (website, social media etc.)	☐
Create AIS	☐
Send AIS to libraries and bookstores	☐
Begin edit	☐
Enlist beta readers or editor	☐
Finish all edits	☐
Register CIP with NLA	☐

Begin book layout ☐

Finish book layout ☐

Finish book cover, front, back and spine ☐

More edits before sending file to printer ☐

Create PDF files for printer ☐

Create ePub file for eBook ☐

Download files with printer ☐

Create preorder forms for potential readers ☐

Organise book launch date/ book venue ☐

Continue marketing ☐

Create press releases/blurbs other marketing ☐

Contact media ☐

Receive book proof ☐

Edits of proof with beta readers/editors ☐

Final edit of proof ☐

Order your first books with printer ☐

Receive books from printer (celebrate) ☐

Sell books ☐

Design marketing swag, bookmarks, banners etc. ☐

Print marketing swag for book launch ☐

Buy other props for book launch ☐

Advertise or market book launch ☐

Book launch ☐

Continue marketing and selling ☐

☐

☐

☐

Chapter Twenty-Three
Keeping records

When I'm in the creative groove (which is most of my life, *yeah, right!*), I tend to put things in odd places, stack folders on the floor, have multiple notebooks (I'm not sure what I wrote in most of them), pens all over the place, stick-it notes on my desk — *a bit of creative chaos.*

I found I was wasting time better spent writing. I'm still working on the perfect setup because I work part-time (like many of us) and need to keep that side separate. I can cope with most of the filing, admin, accounting side, but I needed a system for my writing projects.

Keeping track of the books I sell (personally) has been arduous. If I don't update it regularly, I forget who bought a book. I now keep a notebook for that purpose and later added it to Access.

I use SquareUp for desktop when selling books at launches and signings. This handy payment app keeps track of inventory and sales and links to your bank account.

I make use of Excel spreadsheets for my bookkeeping and book sales (updated from the notebook). I have created templates of these you can download. I also have book purchases (from Ingram) sales (to book buyers) in Access. It's a double-up but works.

I love MYOB for accounting, but it's expensive and complicated for some people. You could use Xero, Quicken, Free Accounting Software, or any program that keeps the money side of your business organised. Some authors like to keep a traditional ledger. There's nothing wrong with that either.

Go back to my Suggested Programs and Apps list on page 88 for more suggestions. It's also a good idea to do a marketing plan and stick to it (I've included a template for that as well). Otherwise, you'll just be promoting haphazardly and getting no results. I use Later.com to schedule my social media posts.

As a published author, you want to spend most of your time writing your stories, not reorganising the office (yep, stop wasting time on Facey). Keep trays for every book or writing job (if you freelance) and put everything in its place.

To be able to find things quickly gives you more time to write. Don't waste time because of an unorganised office. Go to Officeworks, Kmart even Bunnings to find office storage ideas that are inexpensive and look business-like, but more importantly – are functional.

Most of you will keep records on your computer. The Excel and Word files I've given you will help make it easier. They will avoid stressing you out. There will be no dampening your enthusiasm for your writing business.

I want you to love self-publishing. Keep good records, stay organised, and you will flourish.

Chapter Twenty-Four
Future plans

It's essential to set goals and have plans for the future of your self-publishing business. These can be in diary form, on your computer, pinned to your corkboard - anywhere.

Are you happy to only ever publish one book? If that's your dream fulfilled and a tick off the bucket list – great for you.

I would think most of you would say, "No way. I loved publishing my first book. I want to publish more."

So, what now?

You need a plan.

At a writer's signing, one successful author told me her secret to success was publishing something every three months. I know I had my hand over my open mouth too. I thought I was doing okay with a book a year.

Some authors believe you need to keep momentum, especially with Amazon; you need to publish often. A backlist frequently helps future sales. It may mean publishing short stories in-between novels or digging up an old manuscript you didn't publish and reworking it. Don't push yourself. I think quality over quantity is best. But that's just me.

Work at your own pace. Whatever works for you.

Perhaps you have the time and speed to crank out multiple novels a year (or novellas). If you do, go ahead.

Maybe you would be better at plodding along with a book each year or two. That is fine too.

Do you want a blockbuster or two? Every writer's dream and the only way to fulfil it is to try.

Either way, believe it, envision it – write it down as a goal. Make it real.

Use this table or write in your journal:

My goal is	Date to accomplish the goal

Chapter Twenty-Six
The last words

There is so much more you can do in self-publishing than ever before. Less stigma is attached to indie authors, and many are hybrid (meaning they are traditionally and independently published).

It's exciting times for self-published authors. I could write about this topic longer, but I want you to get to work on your self-publishing business. Instead, I give you three more tips and then you're on your own (with this book beside you, of course).

Network with your tribe for the processes you can't do yourself
Writing is a lonely enough job already without adding self-publishing to the mix. Everything is up to you. Often you have no time for family and friends, but you must give yourself a breather. Not only with your nearest and dearest but your people (writers!) Go back and read pages 95-97 about finding your helpers.

To find your people, I suggest you attend conferences. Partake in masterclasses. Follow forums, comment and partake in online groups. Attend signings (the group ones are superb for networking). Arrange get-togethers with other writers, brainstorm, enjoy the banter and take notes.

You'll soon find you have people within the writing industry who can help you self-publish to your best ability. Work on those networks because they are invaluable.

Suggested writers' groups
Here's a small list of my favourite writing-related groups or websites to find your writing people:

ASA	https://www.asauthors.org
Aus Crime Writers	https://www.austcrimewriters.com/
RWA	https://romanceaustralia.com/
Aus Writers Centre	https://www.writerscentre.com.au/
RWZ	http://www.romancewriters.co.nz/
Writers' Digest	https://www.writersdigest.com
The Creative Penn	https://www.thecreativepenn.com
MRWG	http://www.melbournerwg.com/
Now Novel	https://www.nownovel.com
Writer's Relief	http://writersrelief.com/
The Write Life	https://thewritelife.com/
Aust Writers	http://www.austwriters.com
	(includes most Australian writers' groups for each state and territory)

Suggested social media groups
There are so many - this is but the tip of the iceberg.

Romance Writers of Australia Facebook Community Group
https://www.facebook.com/groups/RWACommunity/
Australian and New Zealand Readers/Authors/Bloggers
https://www.facebook.com/groups/344740712322103/
Australian Writers Rock
https://www.facebook.com/groups/393427772952
Writers Around Australia
https://www.facebook.com/groups/1882118278675718/
Creative Fiction Writing
https://www.facebook.com/groups/CreativeFictionWriting/
Authors and Writers Helping each other grow
https://www.facebook.com/groups/1882118278675718/
Australian Romance Readers
https://www.facebook.com/groups/1456723501294615/
Beta Readers and Critiques
https://www.facebook.com/groups/1662819743977604/

Seasoned Romance
https://www.facebook.com/groups/958318970951705/

To stay safe in the tricky world of publishing
Writer's Beware
https://www.facebook.com/WriterBeware

And keep searching to find more.

Now it's up to you.

Dream big. Good luck - now get cracking!

And, when you've self-published your book, I'd love to know about it and share it on the pages of my blog.

Email me at donna@warmwittywords.com.au

Turn over the page to find out about the free templates.

Chapter Twenty-Seven
Free Templates

After joining my mailing list, you'll be able to download the free templates to use in your self-publishing business. Go to the link below:

https://www.subscribepage.com/selfpublishingfree

Once you have the code for the downloads, feel free to return as I add more downloads. Some might be free reads and other advice.

It may seem using my books as exemplars is a shameless plug. Sorry about that. *Ha, ha, sorry, not sorry.* This guide portrays how I published and what I learned during the process. It worked best with my examples (and importantly, I have the copyright). Using screenshots as I produced my books is the best way to convey how self-publishing works.

In the meantime, I'm working on publishing two more fiction manuscripts. Maybe I'll go hybrid this time. Wait and see. And, if you subscribe to the newsletter to get your free templates, you'll never miss the latest exciting news.

When you start your author newsletter, I'll happily join yours. Indie authors should help each other grown. Make a point of supporting your fellow writers, and that backing will come back to you tenfold.

Good luck, have fun, and I wish you much success. 😊

Author Bio

Donna Munro is an Australian author of fiction and non-fiction.

The successful freelance writer was in national publications such as *The Australian Women's Weekly, She, Woman's Day, That's Life,* and *Take 5,* anthologies, and other magazines.

She is the RWA Administrative Assistant, a previous *Hearts Talk* and magazine design editor, graphic artist, newsletter, book and website designer extraordinaire. She helped other writers by ghostwriting four books. In her twenties, she worked on a prawn trawler as a cook. Despite her terrible culinary skills, the crew didn't throw her overboard.

Donna never reached five-foot-tall but don't underestimate this pocket rocket for her shortness. She's addicted to Peanut Butter, follows the Sydney Roosters and loves cheerful, yellow sunflowers.

When not at her desk with a dog snoring beneath it, you'll often find her on a beach. She'll have a book in her hands and her toes in the sand.

Also find her at:

Website www.donnamunroauthor.com
Blog www.warmwittywords.com.au
Facebook www.facebook.com/donnamunrowarmwittywords
Instagram www.instagram.com/donnadmunro
Twitter twitter.com/warmwittywords
Pinterest www.pinterest.com.au/donnawritings
Goodreads www.goodreads.com/author/show/16547319.Donna_Munro
Bookbub www.bookbub.com/profile/donna-munro

Acknowledgements

A big thank you to my long-suffering, non-writing family who put up with vagueness and my long hours on a keyboard (the computer kind, not a piano. I don't have a musical bone in my body).

Special thanks to my real book boyfriend (aka husband), Bevil, who brings me beverages (which may or may not be beer) when I'm still writing after dark.

Thanks, Blake, for the interruptions of worldly insights and deep thoughts. At least you help to keep my mind active.

Thanks, Joel and Kris, for being proud of my writing (though you're yet to read it).

Mum, Dieter, Brad and Kaz and our extended family for always encouraging the publishing dream. Thank you for loving books, Mum, and sharing that passion with me.

I've passed book love onto Larabella and Kru, grandchildren who think it's pretty cool to have a Nanny who's an author.

Thanks to the Ashby's for holding my first ever book launch.

Michelle Somers, you are not only an incredible human but the best kind of successful author who passes on the wisdom. I am forever grateful for your advice about this book (and previous ones). Any success I'll share with you.

Anna Ugrinic for taking my calls about word counts, publishers, agents and other writerly things, always being patient with me and helping me proofread the first proof copy of this book.

Thanks to Vicki Milliken, who missed the course in 2019 but volunteered to read the workbook and give suggestions and corrections.

Thank you to my RWA and Qld Writers, who have given me inspiration and guidance as an author. There are too many people to thank in these organisations. RWA boosts its members, encourage individuality and applaud their successes.

Thanks for teaching me the publishing ropes, Sandra, Bruce, Marilyn and Clive, allowing me to realise I could go it alone.

Thank you to Bevan Ellem, who gave me my first magazine editor gig (*Wax 'n' Wind*) way back in 1988. You encouraged me to write as well as design. I'll never forget my favourite one-armed bookie.

Thank you, my Genrefluent Writers critique group, Lee, Jo and Sally (now onto other pastures), for ever-insightful critiquing, library and lunch catchups. You girls get the writing gig.

Though this book wasn't part of my manuscript development at Sunshine Coast Creative Alliance, I'd like to express gratitude to them for allowing me to join. I wrote a fiction manuscript under the guidance of the fabulous Melanie Myers. Melanie, I'm in debt thanks to your ability to get the best out of my writing.

Thanks, Angie, for being uniquely you, my dear friend. Thank you for meeting me at Bookfests because we both love books. You proofread and bought my books, encouraged me, and shared long walks in Noosa National Park (among other places, like 35 km in one day on the Sunshine Coast). You are a fantastic, beloved friend and survivor. I hope to enjoy many more long walks with you (not 35 km — *no way!*).

I guess the enormous thanks should go to my novel readers. If you're not an aspiring self-publisher, you may never pick up this book, but I thank you for reading my first books and telling me how much you love them. *You all rock!*

Did you enjoy this book?

Did this book help clarify what you need to do to self-publish in Australia? If so, that's terrific. I accomplished what I set out to do.

Reviews are a potent way to draw attention to this book and help other aspiring authors like you. Though I use different marketing strategies, the reviews are the ones I enjoy the most. Feedback from readers creates word-of-mouth, the rawest form of praises and publicity.

Honest reviews are welcome, especially on Amazon, Goodreads, BookBub, Books2Read, Kobo and anywhere you have bought my book.

If you'd prefer to email me your review, send it to donna@warmwittywords.com.au.

Here's the link to Amazon Australia Amazon

Thank you, kind readers, for picking up this book. I hope it sits proudly among your writing references and becomes a valuable tool for your self-publishing business.

Pre-release Reviews

'What a great resource for writers like me who are just starting, or fairly new to the whole writing industry. This book not only includes all the basics of what you need to do, it includes so much more advice on the whole writing process, from editing to marketing and more. This is something I will bring out to re-read parts over and over again.'

- Five-star review by Journalist Sharyn Swanepoel.

'Excellent resource for new authors. Step by step guide on how to publish your book. Concise and to the point with pictures, tables, and diagrams to help you along. So glad I found this book!'

- Five-star review by Nicca.

CPSIA information can be obtained
at www.ICGtesting.com
Printed in the USA
BVHW060012101122
651653BV00007B/68

9 780648 019480